# APPARITIONS

# APPARITIONS

## REVISED EDITION

by G. H. M. Tyrrell

with a Preface by

H. H. PRICE

Collier Books

First Collier Books Edition 1963
Third Printing 1970

This Collier Books edition is published by arrangement with Gerald Duckworth & Co., Ltd.

The Macmillan Company
866 Third Avenue, New York, N.Y. 10022
Printed in the United States of America

This is a question which, after five thousand
years, is still undecided; a question, whether in
theology or philosophy, one of the most important
that can come before the human understanding.
—Dr. Johnson

# Contents

# Preface

APPARITIONS is probably the best of all Tyrrell's writings. One may venture the guess that it will have a place some day among the classics of Psychical Research. A word should first be said about its history. In 1942 Tyrrell was invited to deliver the seventh Myers Memorial Lecture before the Society for Psychical Research. That year happened to be the sixtieth anniversary of the Society's foundation. Accordingly, "it was at first intended that the Lecture should take the form of a general survey of all the work accomplished by the Society since its foundation in so far as that work had yielded positive results. I therefore began with the study of apparitions, because those were the firstfruits of the Society's efforts. After reading a considerable number of cases I was forcibly struck by two things. One was that the evidence provided by these spontaneous narratives was much stronger than I had previously realized; the other was that they throw a veritable searchlight into the workings of human personality. . . . I therefore asked that my terms of reference might be modified so as to allow me to devote the whole of the Lecture . . . to the subject of apparitions alone."[1] The lecture was delivered on October 31, 1942, and was shortly afterwards published by the Society as a pamphlet, which has long been out of print.

The present book, edited by Mr. Edward Osborn, a member of the Council of the Society, is intended for a wider public. Passages referring to the occasion on which the lecture was originally delivered have therefore been omitted. An appendix has also been added, giving a complete list of the principal cases, sixty-one in number, with which Tyrrell il-

[1] These words are quoted from the introductory section of the original lecture (omitted from the present edition).

lustrates his argument; and in the text itself the cases have been re-numbered for easier reference.

The tea-party question, "Do you believe in ghosts?" is one of the most ambiguous which can be asked. But if we take it to mean, "Do you believe that people sometimes experience apparitions?" the answer is that they certainly do. No one who examines the evidence can come to any other conclusion. Instead of disputing the facts, we must try to explain them. But whatever explanation we offer, we soon find ourselves in very deep waters indeed.

The pre-scientific theory of apparitions (if anything so vague can be called a theory) was that an apparition is a *physical* entity, physically present in the room or other place where the percipient is. It was supposed to be a kind of physical duplicate of some human being whose body is many miles away, and perhaps long dead. It is true, of course, that apparitions do have some of the characteristics of ordinary material objects. For instance, they show perspectival changes when they move about. Sometimes (in the so-called "Collective Cases") they are perceived by several people at the same time. Sometimes they are audible as well as visible, or audible to some percipients while they are visible to others. Sometimes, though only very rarely, they are tangible too. Sometimes, though not always, they are reflected in mirrors and cast shadows. On the other hand, they do not seem to be impenetrable. They appear, and later disappear, in a physically inexplicable manner. They do not leave any physical traces behind them, such as footprints. Moreover, the "publicity" which they have is not an unrestricted publicity. If there are three percipients in the room, two of them may see the apparition while the third does not. Or perhaps none of them sees it, but a domestic animal does, or at any rate behaves as if it did. In fact, the difficulties in the way of this physical theory of apparitions are so great that we cannot be surprised if scientifically educated people refuse to "believe in ghosts" at all. Some of them have even maintained that the term "ghost" is a self-contradictory one. It would follow, of course, that any statement of the form "X sees a ghost" *must* always be false.

If a physical theory of apparitions is so unpromising, it is natural to try a psychological one instead. Here we start from the concept of hallucination. We know from other evidence that hallucinations do occur, not only in mental disease or under the influence of drugs, but also occasionally in normal people. To put it crudely, we know from other evidence that it is possible to see or hear "something which is not really there." It must be clearly understood that an hallucination is not just a false belief, though it is often accompanied by a false belief. It is a *percept* or series of percepts. An hallucinated person has sense-experiences, usually visual or auditory, which closely resemble the experiences he would have if a certain physical object were stimulating his sense-organs; but in actual fact, no such physical object is present. Apparitions, however, are hallucinations of a very special kind. They *correspond* pretty closely to some physical object or event external to the percipient's organism, though that object or event is not physically present in the percipient's neighbourhood, and may be many miles away. Thus apparitions differ from the purely subjective hallucinations of the insane or of drug-takers. We may describe them as *telepathic* hallucinations.

In the so-called "crisis-apparition"—the type of case which has been most carefully studied—it does seem pretty clear that the phenomenon is telepathic in origin. At or about the time when a person A is undergoing some crisis (which may or may not be death) another person B, usually a friend or relative, has a visual hallucination; and this may be so complete and lifelike that he at first believes A to be physically present in the room, and is only undeceived when the apparition vanishes. It would seem that such "telepathic phantasms" are just one of the many ways in which an unconsciously received telepathic impression may manifest itself to the recipient's consciousness. (Alternatively, it may manifest itself by means of automatic writing; in the form of a dream, or in waking mental imagery; or in an auditory hallucination instead of a visual one.) In the crisis-apparition a telepathically-received impression makes use of the psycho-physical machinery of hallucination "to get itself across"—to make itself consciously known to the percipient and thereby to influence his emotions and his actions.

But not all apparitions are crisis-apparitions. There are also *post mortem* apparitions.[2] There are haunting apparitions, where the same apparitional figure is seen repeatedly in a particular locality, over a longish period of time. (Haunting is sometimes auditory instead of visual, and occasionally both at once. Sometimes, though rarely, it is olfactory.) Moreover, there are just a few "experimental cases," where one person A, by a deliberate effort of will, has succeeded in causing another person B to experience an apparition of him at a distance. We have also to remember that some apparitions in all four classes are "collective"; that is, the apparition is seen or heard by several percipients at the same time. The telepathic explanation does seem to fit some of the facts very well. Can it be extended to cover all of them? Most students of Psychical Research have assumed, as a working hypothesis at least, that it can. Tyrrell himself shares this assumption. But as he remarks, the telepathic explanation of apparitions, in the form in which it is usually stated, "leaves a great deal unsaid."[3]

His aim in this essay is to say the things which have hitherto been left unsaid. He tries to reformulate the telepathic theory of apparitions in a much more concrete and detailed way, and he tries to meet the obvious objections to it. The clue which he uses is just his conception of Psychical Research itself. In his view, the primary task of Psychical Research was nothing more nor less than "the exploration of human personality," and particularly the exploration of its subliminal or unconscious strata. It was in this region, then, that the explanation of apparitions must be sought. And conversely, he thought that the chief importance of apparitions, as of other supernormal occurrences, was the light they might be expected to throw on the structure of human personality.

If we look at the problem from this point of view, we can

2 *Post mortem* is conventionally taken to mean "more than 12 hours after death." An apparition of a person A is counted as a crisis-apparition if it occurs less than 12 hours after A's death.

3 P. 46 below.

see that the traditional telepathic theory of apparitions does indeed "leave a great deal unsaid." In the crisis-cases, for instance, the telepathic agent need not know exactly where the percipient is, or in just what surroundings, and sometimes he has no means of knowing. Yet the apparition contrives to *adapt* itself to those surroundings, exactly as if it was a real material object standing or moving about among them. Sometimes it is even reflected in a mirror, and sometimes it casts a shadow. As it moves about, it shows appropriate perspectival changes. Even if the agent were very familiar with the room in which the percipient is, how could he possibly know just where the percipient would be in the room when the telepathic impression was received? Yet the apparition looks just as a real material object would look if seen from one quite determinate point of view in space. Again, as has often been pointed out, the agent has only a vague knowledge of what he himself looks like when seen from outside. But the apparition does closely resemble him as he looks when seen from outside, so closely that the percipient at first assumes without hesitation that the man is physically there in the room before his eyes.

Tyrrell concludes from this that what is telepathically "transmitted" can only be a pretty vague and general idea, what he himself calls a *theme* or *motif.* Perhaps the agent merely thinks "I wish X could see me now, wherever he is." This thought may have great emotional intensity, but its intellectual content is very general indeed. Before the apparition can occur, this general theme or motif must somehow be *specified* and made concrete. It must somehow be worked out in detail. And then, further, the details must be actually presented to the percipient's consciousness in the form of a determinate and highly complicated visual hallucination, so arranged that it will fit in with the visible scene which the percipient is aware of at the time. Tyrrell tries to make the situation more comprehensible by using the analogy of a drama. He speaks repeatedly of "the apparitional drama" and this, we may say, is the key-phrase of his theory. As we have seen, the original telepathic impression provides only the general outline of the plot. To work out the details, we must postulate some further entity or factor which Tyrrell calls "the Producer." But even when the apparitional drama has been worked out in detail, the task of *presenting* it still remains. This task is assigned to another entity or factor which Tyrrell calls "the Stage Carpenter." The Stage Carpenter's function is to bring into existence just those hallucinatory percepts which the Producer's plan requires.

The Producer and the Stage Carpenter may be thought of as psychological constituents of the percipient's personality, constituents of it which operate in a quasi-autonomous manner below the level of consciousness. It is natural to suppose that they also operate when we are dreaming, though in normal dreams (i.e. non-telepathic ones) the theme or motif does not come from without, but is provided by some unconscious wish, fear, etc., belonging to the dreamer himself. I fancy we are not as astonished as we should be by the prodigious dramatic power which the dreaming mind possesses, even in the most hard-headed and matter-of-fact persons. This same dramatic power, according to Tyrrell, is shown in apparitions, though the apparitional drama, unlike the dream-drama, is a waking hallucination; and "the Producer" and "the Stage Carpenter" are his rather whimsical names for the unconscious mental factors which are responsible. It is worth while to remember that telepathic impressions do sometimes dramatize themselves in the form of a dream; and it is unfortunate, perhaps, that telepathic dreams were outside Tyrrell's terms of reference in this essay.

The Producer and the Stage Carpenter are what Tyrrell calls *mid-level* constituents of our personalities. The term needs some explanation. Tyrrell conceives of Human Personality as a many-graded hierarchy, in which there are "degrees of I-ness." One's body is in a way "I," but one's thoughts and feelings are "more I" than the body is, and the conscious self[4] is the "most I" thing of all. To the conscious self even its own thoughts and feelings are in a way objects, *other* than it. From its point of view, even thoughts and feelings are in some degree environmental, and the body still more so. Between the conscious self at the one end of the series

[4] The "Conscious Self," as Tyrrell uses the phrase, corresponds more or less to the "Atman" or "Witness" of the classical Hindu philosophers, and to the "Pure ego" of some Western thinkers.

and the body at the other there are many intermediate levels, and that is where the Producer and the Stage Carpenter belong. It is characteristic of these mid-level constituents of personality that they are intermediate between mind and matter, as mind and matter are ordinarily conceived. Tyrrell tries to bring this out by using the curious hyphenated phrase "idea-pattern." What lies behind the apparitional drama, he says, may best be called an idea-pattern. There is something resembling intelligence and purpose in it. Yet it is also like a mere pattern, because it is carried into effect in an automatic and unconscious way. (I am not quite sure what the word "pattern" is intended to convey. Perhaps Tyrrell was thinking of a gramophone record or something of the kind.) He suggests in passing that something of the same hybrid sort, intermediate between an idea and a pattern, may also be responsible for the characteristic phenomena of organic life. If so, "idea-patterns" would be much the same as the "forms" which play a crucial part in the ancient Aristotelian version of vitalistic biology.

As Tyrrell first introduces them, the Producer and the Stage Carpenter are constituents of the *percipient's* personality. But this turns out to be an over-simplification. For the mid-level constituents of one personality, he says, are not wholly separate from the mid-level constituents of another. We began by assuming that the telepathic agent just "transmitted" a bare theme or motif; and that the percipient (or rather the mid-levels of the percipient's personality) did all the rest. But we ought rather to think of a two-sided collaboration between the mid-level constituents of the one personality and the mid-level constituents of the other. What we call telepathy is not literally the transmission of anything. According to Tyrrell, the word "telepathy" is just a way of referring to the *non-separate* character which the mid-levels of different personalities have. In these mid-level strata, the notion of spatial apartness no longer applies. So if I see an apparition of you, the plot of this apparitional drama is the joint result of the joint efforts of your "Producer" and mine.

In the rather silly tea-table conversations to which I referred at the beginning, one sometimes encounters the question "Why do ghosts wear clothes?" As a matter of fact, if the questioner had read the evidence, he might also have asked why "ghosts" are sometimes accompanied by horses and carriages and other apparently physical appurtenances. Tyrrell's theory solves this problem quite easily. The clothes, horses, etc., are as hallucinatory as the "ghost" itself is. They are there because they are required by the "theme" or "motif" of the apparitional drama, just as they would be there in a dream if the theme of the dream-drama required it. They are dramatically appropriate. The same explanation applies to the behaviour of the apparition itself. The door is locked. Yet the apparition opens it and walks into the room. Physically, the door does not move. Its movement is as hallucinatory as the apparition itself is. But the opening of the door is dramatically appropriate, if the theme of the drama is the idea of *going* into the room where Mr. X is. Similarly if the apparition casts a shadow, or is reflected in the mirror, or makes a noise of footsteps as it moves, this is because the Stage Carpenter is efficient at his job. His instructions were to provide as lifelike a representation as possible of what would be seen and heard if the agent were physically present and physically moving about in the room.

The solution of this problem is fairly obvious. But there is another problem which is much more difficult, so difficult that it puzzled investigators of the calibre of Myers and Gurney. As has been mentioned already, apparitions are sometimes *collective;* that is, they are seen or heard by several percipients at the same time. The very existence of collective cases is on the face of it a grave difficulty for any telepathic theory of apparitions. Surely a telepathic hallucination ought to be a purely private phenomenon, experienced only by the person for whom the telepathic communication is intended? But in fact it is sometimes experienced by indifferent bystanders as well. The notion of a *public* hallucination is a very strange one, almost as strange as the notion of a public dream. Shall we not have to suppose, as Myers did, that in these collective cases at any rate the apparition *is* after all a quasi-physical entity, physically present in space in the neighbourhood of the percipients?

Tyrrell solves this problem in a very ingenious way. He applies the same principle as before, the principle of dramatic appropriateness. The bystanders, if there are any, are drawn into the apparitional drama because it is dramatically necessary that they should be. The theme or motif of the drama requires it. The idea in the agent's mind, which started the whole process going, was the quite vague or general idea of being in the place where Mr. X, his friend or relative, is. But *if* the agent really were in that place, and *if* there were other persons present, then he would have to be perceptible to these other persons as well as to X. So if the Producer and the Stage Carpenter know their job, it will be arranged that the apparition is perceptible by all the persons present. It must be remembered that so far as these "mid-level" functions are concerned there is supposed to be no sharp line between one personality and another. If the theme or motif requires it, the apparitional drama can be arranged co-operatively by the mid-level constituents of several different percipients. The result will be a *collective* apparition. Each of the percipients will experience a visual (and/or auditory) hallucination, and these hallucinations will be correlated with each other, just as normal visual percepts are when several people are perceiving the same physical object at the same time.

Perhaps this rough outline of Tyrrell's main argument may be enough to persuade the reader that the questions discussed in this book are of the greatest theoretical interest. Tyrrell himself always insisted that what Psychical Research chiefly needs in the present stage of its development is new explanatory ideas. In this book, the most constructive and original of all his writings, he has put his own percept into practice.

H. H. PRICE

*Oxford*
  *April* 1953

# Abbreviations

## EXAMPLES

*Proc.* viii. 311 = *Proceedings* of the Society for Psychical Research, Volume viii, page 311.

*J.* vi. 230 = *Journal* of the Society for Psychical Research, Volume vi, page 230.

*P.L.* (34) = *Phantasms of the Living,* by E. Gurney, F. W. H. Myers, and F. Podmore, Case 34.

*H.P.* (714) = *Human Personality and its Survival of Bodily Death,* by F. W. H. Myers, Case 714.

Page references are to the original editions of these works.

# Chapter I

## The Census of Hallucinations

THE FIRST WORK of major importance to be undertaken by the Society for Psychical Research, after its inception in 1882, was the Census of Hallucinations.[1] At the International Congress of Experimental Psychology, held in Paris in 1889, the plan of this Census was approved, and the work formally entrusted to Professor Henry Sidgwick. Collaborating with Henry Sidgwick were Miss Alice Johnson, Frederic Myers, Dr. A. T. Myers, Frank Podmore, and Mrs. Sidgwick; and probably this little group could not have been bettered from the point of view of ability, caution, and soundness of judgement. The work was carried out with great thoroughness, and those features likely to be of particular interest to psychologists were given especial prominence.

The main purpose of the Census was to test for evidence of telepathy by questioning a representative sample of the public. This questioning was intended to reveal what proportion of the population experiences sensory hallucinations during hours of wakefulness, particularly of the externalized kind which constitutes an apparition. Further, it was desired to make a full examination of the evidence collected from several points of view in addition to testing it for evidence of telepathy. If hallucinations were found to coincide with external events, clearly corresponding to them oftener than chance would account for, this would provide evidence for a causal connection between the event and the hallucination; and if no normal causal relation could be suggested, the relation would apparently be that of telepathy.

The word "telepathy," meaning literally "feeling at a distance," as used by its originators, was not intended to imply that distance necessarily enters into the telepathic process in the sense that anything literally travels from one person to

[1] *Proc.* x.

another through space. They used the word in a sense which left the possibility open for either a physical or a non-physical explanation. "It has been found convenient to use the term," they say, "for scientific purposes, as merely connoting the exclusion of the recognized channels of sensation, and not necessarily implying any definite interval of space between the persons whose states of mind are telepathically connected." It may be added that since the Census of Hallucinations was carried out, the physical theory of telepathy has become less and less tenable. It might therefore be objected that the word "telepathy," implying some sort of action across space, is misleading. But, even though telepathy is a process which has nothing to do with distance or space, it is true that in the majority of cases the bodies of persons whose minds are connected by it are a considerable distance apart. It does *seem,* therefore, to link people across a distance. The word "telepathy" has now entered the language and found its place in the dictionary and has begun to gather those associations in the public mind which make a word useful. It would surely only introduce confusion to attempt to replace it by a new one.

The first step in the Census of Hallucinations was the circulation of a question, called by the investigators the Census Question, which had been compiled with care to include hallucinations of the three senses of sight, hearing, and touch, and to include only those hallucinations experienced in waking life, dreams being excluded. The question read: "Have you ever, when believing yourself to be completely awake, had a vivid impression of seeing or being touched by a living being or inanimate object, or of hearing a voice; which impression, as far as you could discover, was not due to any external physical cause?" The question was printed at the head of a form on which the person canvassed had only to write Yes or No in answer, and to give his name, address, and occupation. For those answering Yes, another form was provided asking for details of their experiences.

The number of collectors engaged on the Census was 410, and the answers of 17,000 persons were obtained. Of these, 15,316 replied No; and 1,684 replied Yes. Of those answering Yes, there was a distinct preponderance of women over men. The material obtained was analysed from many different points of view, including its relation to age, sex, nationality, and health.

The results showed that 9.9, or nearly 10 per cent, of the 17,000 persons questioned had had sensory hallucinations of the kind described in the question; and if these 17,000 formed a fair sample of the population, it follows that about 10 per cent of the whole population have them. Reasons, which appear cogent, are given for the belief that 17,000 is a sufficient number to form a fair sample, and that however many people were questioned, the proportion having such hallucinations would not differ materially from 10 per cent.

In order to discover whether the hallucinations contained evidence for telepathy, it was, of course, necessary to find out how many of them coincided with corresponding external events, and whether the number so coinciding exceeded the number that might be expected from chance. The only group of cases which appeared to offer the material for a statistical calculation of this sort was the group coinciding with death. If a person had a waking hallucination of a recognized friend at precisely the time when that friend died, a coincidence was provided. The evidence was found to contain a number of such coincidences; but it had to be decided what range of latitude was covered by the term "coincidence," since the hallucination and the death sometimes occurred nearly, but not quite, at the same time. It was decided arbitrarily that if the hallucination occurred during a period of 12 hours before to 12 hours after the death, it should be counted as a coincidence. The investigators then proceeded to argue as follows: "The fact that each of us dies only once, enables us to calculate definitely the probability that that death will coincide with any other given event, such as the recognized apparition of the dying person. Taking as a basis for calculation the average annual death rate for England and Wales for the ten years 1881 to 1890 as given in the Registrar-General's Report for 1890, namely 19.15 per thousand, we get as the probability that any one person taken at random would die on a given day, 19.15 in 365,000 or about 1 in 19,000. This, then, may be taken as the general probability that he will die on the day on which his apparition is seen and recognized, supposing that there is no causal connection between the apparition and the death. We ought therefore to find that out of 19,000 apparitions of living persons, or persons not more than 12 hours dead, one is a death-coincidence."[2]

Certain allowances are then made in the number of death-coincidences occurring in the collected cases for reasons fully discussed, and the conclusion reached that 30 death-coincidences have occurred in 1,300 cases, a proportion of about 1 in 43. "But chance would, as we have seen," the investigators continue, "produce death-coincidences at the rate of 1 in 19,000 apparitions of recognized living persons, and 1 in 43 is equivalent to about 440 in 19,000 or 440 times the most probable number."

For myself, I admit that I am unable to follow this reasoning. When the compilers of the report say, in the extract above, that the death-rate is 19.15 per thousand, they add, "We get as the probability that any one person taken at random would die on a given day, 19.15 in 365,000 or about 1 in 19,000. This, then, may be taken as the general probability that he will die on the day on which his apparition is seen and recognized, supposing that there is no causal connection between the apparition and the death." But the mortality statistics only tell us *what proportion of the population* may be expected to die on a given day. They tell us nothing about particular individuals. The probability that *any one person taken at random* will die on a particular day surely depends, not on death-statistics, but on his own peculiar circumstances, his age and state of health, and so on; so that the above statement as to the probability of "any one person taken at random" dying on a particular day would only be true if every one were *equally likely* to die on a particular day. The condition of equal likelihood is assumed in statistical statements of this sort. For example, if a bag contains 50 black balls and 50 white balls, it is commonly said that the probability of drawing a black ball or a white one out of the bag is equal. But this assumes that the drawer is *equally likely* to draw any ball in the bag on each occasion. If all the black balls had been placed at the bottom of the bag and all the white balls on top of them, this condition would not hold, and it is almost certain that a white ball would be drawn first. For this reason I do not feel able to attach any importance to the numerical conclusion which the compilers of the Report have based on this particular argument. At the same time it does not appear to me that their general conclusion is at fault or that any plausible case can be made out for the view that the death-coindences are due to chance. The considerations set forth below in section 4 are alone sufficient to negative that.

Waking hallucinations of an externalized kind are rare, and another line of statistical argument is open which applies at any rate to cases in which the death-coincidence is fairly close.

For example, a case is given in which a man came out of an upstairs room, in which he had been alone, on to the landing, noting the time as he did so. He saw the apparition of an old lady, dressed like his mother, come out of another room on the same floor and descend the stairs. As he watched the figure going down, his wife came up the stairs, and passed so close to the descending figure that she appeared to him to brush against it. But she had neither seen nor felt it. At precisely the same time the percipient's mother, dressed in outdoor clothes as the figure had been, died in another town. The Society's Literary Committee, who supplied this case, made the following calculation with regard to chance-coincidence. "Let us say that the percipient has had only 30 years of intelligent life, and that during those 30 years he has slept for 9 hours a day. He has then had $15 \times 30 \times 365 = 164,250$ hours of waking, intelligent life. Now, in this space of time, he has had *one* apparition, which resembled his mother and was within a few minutes of her death. Now, if we say only that it was within the quarter of an hour in which death occurred, there are $164,250$ hours $= 657,000$ quarter-hours of life in which that apparition might have come; so that the chance of its coming in the right quarter-hour was $1/657,000$ (keeping to round numbers). But this is on the supposition that the only apparition which could possibly appear to him would be his mother's, or at least one which resembled his mother in general aspect as nearly as the phantom which he actually saw.

"Now, visual hallucinations known to be morbid are by no means limited to the human shape; they are grotesquely varied in ways too numerous to mention. But, for the sake of argument, we are willing to assume (it is a monstrous assumption) that *one-tenth* of all phantoms accidentally caused are likely to resemble a lady in a black bonnet and shawl. The chance, then, that an apparition of the right class (the old lady class) would show itself in the right quarter-hour (the quarter-hour of actual decease) will be $1/657,000 \times 10$; or the chances *against* this happening to any given person will be over $6\frac{1}{2}$ millions to one. That is to say, in order to explain satisfactorily Mr. B's experience on the supposition of accidental coincidence, it ought to be shown that there are something like $6\frac{1}{2}$ million adult Englishmen now living who have had one single visual hallucination of a very distinct sort in the course of their lives.

"Even if Mr. B's case stood alone, this result would be somewhat surprising. Of course it does *not* stand alone; and if we take from our store, say, only nine more cases of equally close coincidence attending an apparition seen by an English adult now living and not otherwise subject to hallucinations . . . we increase the improbability tenfold and require that 65,000,000 English adults now living should have had a single distinct hallucination, to make it probable that in these ten cases the coincidence would have accidentally occurred as it did."[3]

The weakness of statistics when applied to spontaneous cases is that they are unable to deal with qualitatively complex events in any satisfactory manner. For statistics, events must be assumed to be qualitatively simple, whether they are or not, the ideal events for experimental telepathy being numbers or simple diagrams. But apparitions contain, not only complex detail, but also accompanying subjective feelings and experiences which do not occur at other times, and which therefore are relevant to the statistical calculation, but cannot be taken into account. A single apparitional coincidence, rich

[3] *Proc.* ii. 53-5.

in qualitative detail, would probably be sufficient to dispose of the theory of chance-coincidence if all this detail could be taken into account. Perhaps the best that can be said for statistical methods when they cease to deal with simple events such as cards, etc., is that whatever numerical result they show is bound to be heavily weighted in favour of the chance theory. But it is quite possible that the numerical result may be so far from stating anything relevant to the facts as to be merely misleading.

Several interesting facts emerge from the analysis of the Census of Hallucinations. One is that hallucinations tend to be forgotten with the passage of time. This fact emerges from a table in which the hallucinations are divided up according to the length of time ago when they occurred. The longer the time ago the fewer the hallucinations. Another fact strikingly shown is that although apparitions correspond to other events besides death, they cluster about the moment of death, which is the most conspicuous source of them. They fall off as one passes away from the moment of death, both before and after it. With telepathic apparitions, visual hallucinations are the commonest, whereas in the subjective hallucinations of the insane (the most prominent source of purely subjective hallucinations available to the investigators), auditory hallucinations are the commonest. Foreigners gave a higher percentage of affirmative answers to the Census Question than English people. There is nothing to show that telepathic hallucinations have any connection with morbidity or ill health; they are quite different in character from the hallucinations occurring in delirium or illness. It was rare for any percipient to say that he had had more than one or two experiences of the kind in his life; and 66 per cent of those giving first-hand accounts of their experiences had only had one such experience in the course of their lives.

Much care was devoted to the question of the trustworthiness of the accounts. The possibility of an illusion being mistaken for a hallucination was considered; also the intelligence and educational status of the percipients were taken into account, and the effect of expectancy where it could have applied. The following possible sources of error were also considered. (1) Inaccuracies in the narratives. This is a matter to be decided by individual judgement after each case has been studied separately; but the most effective answer to this question is supplied by the group-characteristic discussed in Ch. II, §10. (2) The possibility that the collectors may have selected death-cases by going to persons they knew had had them. It is shown that at any rate in many of the cases the collectors knew nothing about the percipients' previous experiences before issuing the Census Question. (3) The possibility that expectation, or some other normal cause, may account for the coincidence. This was carefully considered, and the question of expectancy is referred to in Section 1, Case 1 below. More than sufficient weight seems to have been attached to it.

It was, of course, suggested at the time that the collectors might have been hoaxed. Gurney points out with regard to this suggestion that a hoax in answering the Census Question would not have been a particularly exhilarating joke, since the reply had only to be Yes or No. Would the hoaxer have said that he had had an experience when he had not, or the other way about? It seems most probable that he would have said Yes when he should have said No. But that would have had the effect of increasing the number of Yeses, and therefore of increasing the probability that the coincidences were due to chance. The effect of hoaxing, if it ever occurred, must have been negligible.

Figures are given with regard to the collective percipience of telepathic hallucinations. Out of a total of 1,087 visual hallucinations, 95 were collectively perceived, or roughly 9 per cent. But out of the total of 1,087 cases there were only 283 in which another person (or persons) besides the percipient were present. Of these 283, 95 were collectively perceived and 188 were not. This shows that collective percipience does not take place (perhaps naturally) when the percipient is alone at the time of his experience. But when he is not alone, it takes place in about one third of the cases.

In the case of auditory hallucinations, out of a total of 493, 34 were collective, or roughly 7 per cent. But out of the total of 493 cases, there were only 94 in which another person (or persons) besides the percipient were present. Therefore, again, when the percipient is not alone, about one third of the cases are collective.

The compilers of the Report are distrustful of collective hallucinations which occurred out of doors on account of the risk of mistaken identity. Perhaps they are unduly distrustful, for Gurney gives the impression of being somewhat embarrassed by the fact of collective percipience, and not too sure of the theory he advances to explain it. He is, therefore, I think, a little inclined to underestimate the evidence for it.

With regard to the evidence afforded by the Census of Hallucinations for communication with the dead, a number of cases which might be regarded as supporting this interpretation are given for the reader to form his own judgement. "We have found," say the compilers of the Report, "that the distribution of recognized apparitions before, at, and after the death of the person seen affords some argument for the continuity of psychical life and the possibility of communication from the dead. . . . The amount of evidence, however, does not appear to us to constitute anything like a conclusive case for *post-mortem* agency."

At the Second International Congress of Experimental Psychology, held in London in 1892, Professor Henry Sidgwick read an abridgement of the Report, and in the discussion that followed, members of the Congress appeared to hold the view that anyone experiencing a hallucination of the human form must, *ipso facto*, be in a morbid state, although there is nothing in the Report to indicate this. There does not seem to have been any appreciation on the part of the psychologists present at the Congress of the theoretical importance of the work which the Census Committee had performed. Some discussion of the methods and results of the Census Committee was, however, included in a book by a German psychologist, Herr von Edmund Parish, entitled *Ueber die Trugwahrnehmung (Hallucination and Illusion)*, published in Leipzig in 1894.

Parish considers not only the English Census of Hallucinations but also the results of similar inquiries which were carried out at the same time in France, Germany, and the United States. The results of these inquiries together yielded 27,329 answers to the Census Question, 11.96 per cent of which were in the affirmative. Parish thought that the collectors had selected persons likely to give affirmative answers to the questions, although, if this had been the case, it would have *increased,* and not *decreased,* the probability that the coincidental cases were due to chance. His main contention appears to have been that the coincidences revealed by the Census were due to chance because, (1) he assumed that there existed a far larger number of non-coincidental hallucinations than the Census figures show, maintaining that many non-coincidental cases are forgotten by those who experience them; and because (2) most of the coincidental cases reported never occurred since in their case memory worked the other way and supplied false recollections of fictitious events. Thus he supposed that the memories of percipients worked in two opposite ways in the two classes of cases, so as to oblige the chance theory which he wished to maintain. When a critic sees a chance of explaining away psychical phenomena by making either of two contradictory assumptions, one understands that he is in a quandary. But it is surely a bold solution to make *both* the contradictory assumptions at once! The many instances in which the percipient took action on the hallucination (supposed to be a false memory) before the coincidental event was known are, of course, left unexplained. Parish's so-called "criticism" seems to be no more than a desperate struggle to escape from the facts. So far as I am aware, no detailed criticism of a reasonable kind has been made by any adverse critic of the Census results up to date.

## 1. VALUE OF THE EVIDENCE

After the Census of Hallucinations, a steady influx of spontaneous cases was received by the Society for Psychical Research. The weaknesses of spontaneous evidence have often been pointed out, and were thoroughly realized by the collectors themselves. The chief factors with regard to which the collectors were on their guard were the following. They asked: (1) Is the account first hand? (2) Was it written or told before the event was known? (3) Has the principal witness been corroborated? (4) Was the percipient awake at the time? (5) Was the percipient an educated person and of good character? (6) Was the apparition recognized? (7) Was it seen out of doors? (8) Was the percipient anxious or in a state of expectancy? (9) Could relevant details have been read back into the narrative after the event? (10) Could the coincidence between the experience and the event be accounted for by chance?

It is evident that the value attached to a spontaneous case will depend enormously on individual judgement; anyone with a bias against such evidence will find plenty of ways in which he may attempt to explain it away. It is also possible to put before the reader one's own assessment of the evidence and its significance, leaving it to him to read the quoted cases and form his own judgement. It is impossible to discuss in full the evidential value of any case within the limits imposed by the present survey.

My own personal view is that the first-hand testimony of a reasonable witness is, on the whole, trustworthy unless special circumstances, such as the devices of a conjurer or prolonged strain on the attention, have been imposed on the witness. Second-hand evidence by reliable people, though less accurate than first-hand, is by no means valueless. There are probably inaccuracies in many of the narratives contained in the Society's collection; indeed some of the inaccuracies appear, but in my opinion they do not invalidate the evidence as a whole to any serious extent. Another way of stating this is to say that the seven characteristics of apparitions defined below are, in my opinion, observed facts in nature and not inventions or misdescriptions. This opinion is based partly on the evidential value of each case taken separately, but still more on the fact that the seven characteristics are *group-characteristics*.

The conclusions drawn by the compilers of the Census of Hallucinations, and of the spontaneous evidence as a whole, seem to be sober and weighted in favour of normal explanations. Thus, an account is referred to of a certain Mrs. Barter, who dreamed at the time of the Indian Mutiny that she saw her husband wounded and binding up his leg with a puggaree, when four men lifted him and carried him away. The facts ascertained afterwards were that this happened, and that four men did carry him to safety; but he bound up his leg with a black silk neck-tie instead of with a puggaree. On account of this, and of the fact that Mrs. Barter had also had a non-veridical dream about her husband, the case was rejected as evidence for telepathy.[4]

CASE 1[5] Heavy discount was also made if the percipient was in a state of anxiety or expectancy. In one instance a lady staying with a friend was so strongly impressed with the sense of impending calamity at home that she packed her boxes and sat waiting for a telegram to summon her home. The telegram duly arrived announcing that her grandchild had been taken ill, although the child had been perfectly well when she left home. Gurney dismisses this case as evidence for telepathy on the ground that "those who watch over the health of young children are often, of course, in a more or less chronic state of nervousness."

CASE 2 On the other hand, we find a case in which expectancy, raised to a high pitch, does not produce the result it is supposed to. A friend of the percipient's in this case was so seriously ill that his death was expected at any time. The percipient had a dream in which she saw a corpse laid out on the bed, but it was not the corpse of her sick friend but of his wife. The wife, so far as she knew, was not ill; but next day a letter arrived announcing the wife's sudden illness and, later in the day, a telegram announcing her death.

Whenever possible, corroborative evidence for the cases has been obtained and, adds Gurney, we have "excluded all narratives where, on personal acquaintance with the witnesses, we felt we should be uneasy in confronting them with a critical cross-examiner, and we have frequently thought it right to exclude cases otherwise satisfactory that depended on the reports of uneducated persons." The published cases are therefore the cream skimmed from a much larger number.

A point often forgotten in the criticism of psychical phenomena is that, if serious criticism is being attempted, it is not enough to say in a general way that the evidence is insufficient to support a supernormal conclusion. Where a large number of carefully sifted and well-documented cases

[4] P.L. I. p. 337.
[5] References to numbered cases are given in the Appendix.

are concerned, this negative treatment is not enough. It is necessary also to show that some normal explanation *will* reasonably fit each case. I cannot do better than quote Gurney's words on this subject. "The narratives are very various," he says, "and their force is derived from very various characteristics; the endeavour to account for them without resorting to telepathy must, therefore, be carried through a considerable number of groups, before it produces its legitimate effect on the mind. That effect arises from the number and variety of the improbable suppositions, now violent, now vague—contradictory of our experience of all sorts of human acts and human relations—that have to be made at every turn. Not only have we to assume such an extent of forgetfulness and inaccuracy about simple and striking facts of the immediate past as is totally unexampled in any other range of experience. Not only have we to assume that distressing or exciting news about another person produces a havoc in the memory which has never been noted in connection with distress or excitement in any other form. We must leave this merely general ground, and make suppositions as detailed as the evidence itself. We must suppose that some people have a way of dating their letters in indifference to the calendar, or making entries in their diaries on the wrong page and never discovering the error; and that whole families have been struck by the collective hallucination that one of their members had made a particular remark the substance of which had never even entered that member's head; and that it is a recognized custom to write mournful letters about bereavements which have never occurred; and that when A describes to a friend how he has distinctly heard the voice of B, it is not infrequently by a slip of the tongue for C; and that when D says he is not subject to hallucinations of vision, it is through momentary forgetfulness of the fact that he has a spectral illusion once a week; and that when a wife interrupts her husband's slumbers with words of distress or alarm it is only her fun, or a sudden morbid craving for undeserved sympathy; and that when people assert that they were in sound health, in good spirits and wide awake at a particular time which they had occasion to note, it is a safe conclusion that they were having a nightmare, or were the prostrate victims of nervous hypochondria. Every one of these improbabilities is, perhaps, in itself a possibility; but as the narratives drive us from one desperate expedient to another, when time after time we are compelled to own that deliberate falsification is less unlikely than the assumptions we are making, and then again when we submit the theory of deliberate falsification to the cumulative test, and see what is involved in the supposition that hundreds of persons of established character known to us for the most part and unknown to one another, have simultaneously formed a plot to deceive us—there comes a point where the reason rebels. Common sense persists in recognizing that when phenomena, which are united by a fundamental characteristic and have every appearance of forming a single, natural group, are presented to be explained, an explanation which multiplies causes is improbable, and an explanation which multiplies improbable causes becomes, at a certain point, incredible."[6]

One other point occurs. Much of the evidence is old. For some reason or other the supply of spontaneous cases has declined in recent years and the bulk of them date from the latter half of the nineteenth century.[7] It may be felt that such old evidence cannot be good. In answer, however, it is surely true that whatever evidential value it had when it was printed must be the same now. It would be absurd to suggest that the effect on evidence, when it lies in print for a number of years, is that it becomes "corked"!

A more serious objection to spontaneous cases is that several of them were not received and printed until some years after the events related, and by no means always were there any contemporary written records. It seems at first sight, therefore, as if these cases might be ascribed to faulty memory on the part of the narrators and of those who were told about the events, or participated in them, at the time. But anyone who holds this view has to account for the facts about apparitions described in Ch. II, §10. When the rarity

[6] *P.L.* pp. 163-4.

[7] These cases are still reported to the Society for Psychical Research but are less plentiful. Probably as many occur, but people nowadays do not trouble to report them.

of crisis-apparitions is remembered, and their extraordinarily impressive character, accurate memory regarding them becomes less surprising.

## 2. THE "FAGGOT" THEORY

Probably not one of the cases in the spontaneous class is perfect evidence, and this fact has given rise to two views regarding the evidential value of the class as a whole. One view is that if no case is evidentially perfect, then every case is capable of receiving a normal explanation; and therefore, as members of a group, the cases do not support one another. The sum of any number of zeroes, the advocates of this view say, is still zero. The other view is that, although each case is imperfect, the sum of their evidence is cumulative, and together they support one another, like a number of sticks, each individually weak, but which together form a strong faggot.

It is evidently necessary to decide between these two views before troubling to collect and examine spontaneous evidence; for if the first is the true view, no number of cases has any evidential value whatever unless at least one theoretically flawless case is included. Even then there is no guarantee that everybody will agree as to what constitutes a theoretically flawless case. It is also clear that if the advocates of the first view are right, very little valid evidence can exist on any subject whatever. I suggest that the dilemma arises from dividing evidence into two false classes, or at least into two classes which have no relevance to practical experience, namely the perfect and the imperfect. This division is theoretical. We do not find evidence of this theoretically perfect kind, which raises probability in one jump to dead certainty. All the evidence we come across in real life is faulty to a greater or less extent; and the only question of importance is *how good* the evidence is; not whether it is perfect or imperfect. Evidence is a matter of degree.

Since we are bound in this imperfect world to deal with evidence which falls short of theoretical perfection, the question of whether or not cases may rightly be regarded as forming a faggot would seem to depend on the standard of evidence which they reach individually. If the sticks have any strength in them at all, they will be to some extent stronger collectively than singly. But if every stick is entirely rotten, then the faggot will be just as rotten as the individual sticks. If our cases fall below a certain standard, then the second view will be the correct one. But if they are above a certain standard, the first view will be the correct one. It is true that it is not easy to draw an exact line defining the required standard; but I think one may say generally that first-hand cases from reasonable witnesses, and a good many high standard second-hand cases, are above the line. Third-hand cases and hearsay evidence are below it; for the latter may, as a rule, if not always, be reasonably given a normal explanation; and then the no-mutual-support argument holds. On the other hand, cases above the line may possess evidential imperfections and yet contribute to the evidence. An example will illustrate this.

The percipient in this case, a child of ten, was walking along a country lane near her home, reading a book on geometry. Quite suddenly her surroundings faded away and she saw her mother lying on the floor of a disused room in her home, known as the White Room, apparently dead; and beside her lay a lace-bordered handkerchief. So real was the vision that instead of going home she went straight to the house of the doctor and took him home with her. There they found the child's mother, lying on the floor of the White Room (an unlikely place for her to be), suffering from a bad heart attack, and the handkerchief seen in the vision lay beside her. The doctor was just in time to save her life.[8]

The evidence is first hand by the percipient and the father and mother both corroborate it. But it must be admitted that it is not a theoretically perfect case. No record of the child's experience was made before the facts were verified, and therefore it could be said that the details about the unlikely room in which the mother was found and the lace handkerchief on the floor were read back into the story afterwards. But even if this were the case, the fact remains that the child acted on her vision, brought the doctor, and saved her mother's life; and this is evidence of telepathy. The case is

[8] P.L. (20).

an example of an evidentially imperfect narrative which yet forms a true stick in a faggot. It seems fairly safe to conclude that cases which reach the standard required for publication by the Society for Psychical Research are genuinely faggot-building cases.

### 3. THE CASES FORM A NATURAL GROUP

A very important characteristic of spontaneous cases, emphasized by Gurney but perhaps not very generally appreciated, is that they form a natural group. Later, when the various features of the cases have been examined and put together, it will be seen still more clearly how important this group-characteristic is from the point of view of the strength of the evidence. It consists in the fact that the apparitions described in all the narratives agree in presenting certain features and in not presenting others. As Gurney puts it: "Why should not such apparitions hold prolonged converse with the waking friend? Why should they not produce *physical* effects—shed tears on the pillow and make it wet, open the door and leave it open, or leave some tangible token of their presence? It is surely noteworthy that we have not had to reject, on grounds like these, a single narrative which on other grounds would have been admitted. Have all our informants drawn an arbitrary line, and all drawn the same arbitrary line, between the mistakes and exaggerations of which they *will* be guilty, and the mistakes and exaggerations of which they will *not?*"

Assuming that Gurney is right, he is stating that the cases possess a *group-characteristic*. This group-characteristic shows three important things: (1) In so far as it is common to the four classes of apparitions, experimental, crisis-cases, post-mortem cases and ghosts, it suggests that all four classes are the same type of phenomenon. (2) It shows that whatever inaccuracies the narratives contain, they must be reliable in their main essentials, since nothing but a description of the truth could bring about this particular kind of convergence. (3) It supports the "faggot" theory; for the opponents of the "faggot" theory regard the stories as independent inventions; whereas this group-characteristic shows that such independent inventions would not thus converge. This group-characteristic, in fact, even without the support of a statistical calculation, places the whole group of spontaneous cases at once on a high evidential level, as will be seen more clearly in the light of the "perfect apparition," dealt with in Ch. II, §9.

## 4.   CRISIS-CASES AND CHANCE-COINCIDENCE

The calculations relating to chance-coincidence, worked out by the originators of the Census of Hallucinations, can only be regarded as a rough guide. Perhaps the most important thing about them is that they are bound to err on the safe side. The following points must be borne in mind in considering the possibility that the crisis-coincidences are due to chance.

(1) Gurney has reckoned many cases in which no coincidental crisis is discernible as being purely subjective. There is no certainty that these cases are subjective, and there are features about some of them which suggest the contrary; the feature, for example, of collective percipience. The class of subjective hallucinations has therefore probably been assumed by him to be a good deal larger than it is.

(2) "Coincidence" between an apparition and a crisis has been defined as occurrence within a period of 12 hours on either side of the crisis. But a large number of coincidences are much closer than this, and if this fact had been allowed for, the anti-chance probability would have been higher.

(3) In the numerical estimate, the only crisis taken into account is death. All those cases in which the crisis was not death have been ignored.

(4) A fair proportion of the cases were collectively perceived. It is obvious that the probability of two or more percipients having similar hallucinations at the same moment corresponding to the same distant event and very closely, if not exactly, similar to one another is enormously less than the probability of one percipient having such a hallucination alone. In some auditory cases as many as five percipients have shared the experience.

(5) A feature common to a considerable proportion of

the experimental and crisis-cases is their uniquely impressive effect on the percipient. This feature is not appreciated unless a fairly large number of cases is read. But its significance for the theory of chance-coincidence is important. It even becomes a question whether the proposition that this class is due to chance can be given an intelligible meaning.

(6) The whole group of apparitions, in all its four classes, at least as regards the material coming within the scope of the present survey, is found to possess the group-characteristic just mentioned.

It is not perhaps very likely that anyone will attempt to defend the view seriously that crisis-coincidences are due to chance; and I know of no case in which it has been done in detail, although chance is often suggested as an explanation in a vague way. A more plausible explanation, at first sight, seems to be the suggestion that the narratives are unreliable. Curiously enough, this, on account of the group-characteristic mentioned in (6), turns out in the end to be a chance-explanation too, only in another form. Instead of the probability that an apparition coincides by chance with an external event, it turns on the probability that a large number of people, drawing on their imaginations, will happen, independently and by pure chance, to describe the same type of apparition. More will be said on this point later.

The main conclusion emerging from our examination of the spontaneous cases is that chance cannot reasonably be held to explain them, and that no one in the course of half a century has ever demonstrated in a serious and detailed manner that it is a reasonable explanation.

## 5. CLASSES OF APPARITIONS

Apparitions divide themselves into four main classes: (1) Experimental cases, in which the agent has deliberately tried to make his apparition visible to a particular percipient. (2) Cases in which a recognized apparition is seen, heard, or felt at a time when the person represented by the apparition is undergoing some crisis. These cases will be briefly referred to as "Crisis-cases" or "Crisis-apparitions." (3) Cases in which a recognized apparition is seen or heard so long after the death of the person represented by the apparition that no coincidence with any crisis, such as the death of the person, can be supposed. These will be referred to as "Post-mortem cases." (4) Ghosts, or apparitions, which habitually haunt certain places.

The classes are not very sharply differentiated. There are some cases which do not clearly belong to any class, as, for example, unrecognized figures seen on only one occasion; or recognized figures of living people, which do not coincide with any crisis in their lives.

In his historic work, *Phantasms of the Living,* Edmund Gurney included all examples of the first two classes under the title of his book. But crisis-apparitions are not always of living persons, for the crisis is often death, and the apparition in a number of cases is not seen until some hours after death. Gurney decided to reckon all apparitions which *coincided* with the crisis of death as phantasms of the living, and the question then arose as to what constituted coincidence. Since apparitions are clustered about the moment of death, some exactly coinciding with it, some occurring a little before and some a little after, it becomes necessary to draw an arbitrary line defining what constitutes coincidence with death. Gurney drew this line at 12 hours before to 12 hours after death, considering all apparitions occurring within this 24-hour period as being coincident with death. Those which occurred in the 12-hour period after death were considered to have been telepathically received while the agent was still alive and to have been deferred in emergence.

It may be as well to give an abridged specimen of each class of case, so that the reader may have in his mind a representative picture of each of the four classes. Cases cited for illustrative purposes will be given in shortened form, and no attempt will be made to give the full details of the evidence on which they rest.

CASE 3 (Experimental Case.) "On Friday, December 1st, 1882, at 9:30 p.m., I went into a room alone and sat by the fireside, and endeavoured so strongly to fix my mind upon the interior of a house at Kew . . . in which resided Miss V. and her two sisters, that I seemed to be actually in the house. During this experiment I must have fallen into a mesmeric sleep, for although I was conscious, I could not move my limbs. I did not seem to have lost the power of moving them, but I could not make the effort to do so, and my hands, which lay loosely on my knees, about six inches apart, felt involuntarily drawn together and seemed to meet, although I was conscious that they did not move.

"At 10 p.m. I regained my normal state by an effort of the will, and then took a pencil and wrote down on a sheet of note-paper the foregoing statements. When I went to bed on this same night, I determined that I would be in the front bedroom of the above-mentioned house at 12 p.m.,[9] and remain there until I had made my spiritual presence perceptible to the inmates of that room.

"On the next day, Saturday, I went to Kew to spend the evening, and met there a married sister of Miss V. [Namely Mrs. L. The narrator had only met this lady once before.] In the course of conversation (although I did not think for a moment of asking her any questions on such a subject), she told me that on the previous night she had seen me distinctly on two occasions. She had spent the night at Clarence Road and had slept in the front bedroom. At about half-past nine she had seen me in the passage going from one room to another, and at 12 p.m., when she was wide awake, she had seen me enter the bedroom and walk round to where she was sleeping,[10] and take her hair (which is very long) into my hand. She also told me that the apparition took hold of her hand, and gazed intently into it, whereupon she spoke, saying, 'You need not look at the lines, for I have never had any trouble.' She then awoke her sister, Miss V., who was sleeping with her and told her about it. After hearing this account, I took the statement, which I had written down on the previous evening, from my pocket, and showed it to some of the persons present, who were much astonished although incredulous. . . . I asked Mrs. L. if she was not dreaming at the time of the latter experience,

[9] Here and in the next paragraph the narrator clearly means "12 midnight."

[10] The narrator evidently refers to the bed in which she was lying awake.

but this she stoutly denied, and stated that she had forgotten what I was like, but seeing me so distinctly she recognized me at once." The lady and her sister give their corroboration.

Intense concentration by the agent before going to sleep is mentioned in other cases of this kind.

Two features to be noticed about this case are: (i) the agent's figure is seen walking down the passage very much as a figure is often seen in cases of haunting, and (ii) the agent's figure approaches the percipient's bed and behaves with apparent consciousness of her, very much as a crisis-apparition behaves.

The similarity between this experimental case and the spontaneous cases discussed below is obvious. I have found records of 16 occasions on which this experiment has been tried with success, and in most cases success has been achieved on the first attempt. Here, then, is a repeatable experiment, which for some reason or other appears to have been ignored by investigators. It is clearly an important experiment, for if it could be repeated at will, it would enable apparitions to be manufactured. It would be known when and where to expect them, and one could be prepared with the means for testing them—with cameras, sound-recording apparatus or the like. Moreover, the state of the agent could be studied; hypnosis and suggestion could be applied and so on. On several of the recorded occasions the agent, after concentrating his mind strongly on the selected percipient (who was ignorant that any experiment was being tried), went to sleep; and it was while he was asleep that the apparition was seen.

Mr. J. Kirk (*J.* v. 21-30) made nine successful experiments (only one of which has been counted in the above sixteen, because on only one occasion was his apparition actually seen), and these are of great interest, because they bridge the gap between experimental apparitions and experimental telepathy. For example, in one experiment Mr. Kirk, instead of trying to make his own apparition seen, tried to make the percipient see a bright disc at which he was looking. She saw luminous clouds which concentrated into a disc.

CASE 4 (Crisis Case.) The percipient's half-brother (she refers to him as her brother), an airman, had been shot down in France on the 19th March, 1917, early in the morning. She herself was in India. "My brother," she says, "appeared to me on the 19th March, 1917. At the time I was either sewing or talking to my baby—I cannot remember quite what I was doing at that moment. The baby was on the bed. I had a very strong feeling that I must turn round; on doing so I saw my brother, Eldred W. Bowyer-Bower. Thinking he was alive and had been sent out to India, I was simply delighted to see him, and turned round quickly to put baby in a safe place on the bed, so that I could go on talking to my brother; then turned again and put my hand out to him, when I found he was not there. I thought he was only joking, so I called him and looked everywhere I could think of looking. It was only when I could not find him I became very frightened and had the awful fear that he might be dead. I felt very sick and giddy. I think it was 2 o'clock the baby was christened and in the church I felt he was there, but I could not see him. Two weeks later I saw in the paper he was missing. Yet I could not bring myself to believe he had passed away."

This illustrates, simply, two common features of crisis-apparitions. (i) That they are so like human beings as to be frequently mistaken for them, until they vanish. (ii) That they do not occur when people are expecting them, or because people are worried or anxious about the agent. They usually burst in upon them while they are engaged in their ordinary occupations, or while they are lying in bed.

CASE 5 (Post-mortem Case.) Mrs. P. and her husband had gone to bed, but she, wrapped in her dressing-gown, was lying on the outside of the bed, waiting to attend to her baby, which lay in a cot beside her. The lamp was still alight and the door of the room was locked. She says, "I was just pulling myself into a half sitting posture against the pillows, thinking of nothing but the arrangements for the following day, when, to my great astonishment I saw a gentleman standing at the foot of the bed, dressed as a naval officer, and with a cap on his head having a projecting peak. The light being in the position which I have indicated, the face was in shadow *to me,* and the more so that the visitor was leaning upon his arms which rested on the foot rail of the bedstead. I was too astonished to be afraid, but simply wondered who it could be; and instantly touching my husband's shoulder (whose face was turned from me), I said, 'Willie, who is this?' My husband turned, and, for a second or two, lay looking in intense astonishment at the intruder; then, lifting himself a little, he shouted, 'What on earth are you doing here, sir?' Meanwhile the form, slowly drawing himself into an upright position, now said, in a commanding yet reproachful voice, 'Willie, Willie!' I looked at my husband and saw that his face was white and agitated. As I turned towards him he sprang out of bed as though to attack the man, but stood by the bedside as if afraid, or in great perplexity, while the figure calmly and slowly moved *towards the wall* at right angles with the lamp in the direction of the dotted line. [A diagram is included with the account.] As it passed the lamp, a deep shadow fell upon the room as of a material person shutting out the light from us by his intervening body, and he disappeared, as it were, into the wall. My husband now, in a very agitated manner, caught up the lamp and, turning to me, said, 'I mean to look all over the house and see where he is gone.' I was by this time exceedingly agitated too, but, remembering that the door was locked, and that the mysterious visitor had not gone towards it at all, remarked, 'He has not gone out by the door!' But without pausing, my husband *unlocked* the door, hastened out of the room, and was soon searching the whole house."

Mrs. P. was wondering if the apparition could indicate that her brother, who was in the Navy, was in some trouble, when her husband came back and exclaimed, "Oh no, it was my father!" She continues, *"My husband's father had been dead fourteen years:* he had been a naval officer in his young life."

During the following weeks Mr. P. became very ill and then disclosed to his wife that he had got into financial difficulties and, at the time of the apparition, was inclined to take the advice of a man who would probably have ruined him.

Here, again, the figure is like-like and intrudes on the

percipients suddenly and unexpectedly. There is in fact no intrinsic difference between it and a crisis-apparition.

CASE 6 (Ghost.) The percipient, her husband and step-daughter and two small children, with servants, lived in a detached house, which was not more than twenty years old. "We had been there about three weeks," she says, "when, about eleven o'clock one morning, as I was playing the piano in the drawing-room, I had the following experience: I was suddenly aware of a figure peeping round the corner of the folding doors to my left; thinking it must be a visitor, I jumped up and went into the passage, but no one was there, and the hall door, which was half glass, was shut. I only saw the upper half of the figure, which was that of a tall man with a very pale face and dark hair and moustache. The impression lasted only a second or two, but I saw the face so distinctly that to this day I should recognize it if I met it in a crowd. It had a sorrowful expression. It was impossible for anyone to come into the house without being seen or heard. . . . In the following August one evening about 8:30, I had occasion to go into the drawing-room to get something out of the cupboard, when, on turning round, I saw the same figure in the bay window, in front of the shutters, which were closed. I again saw only the upper part of the figure, which seemed to be in a somewhat crouching posture. The light on this occasion came from the hall and the dining-room and did not shine directly on the window; but I was able perfectly to distinguish the face and the expression of the eyes. . . . Later in the same month I was playing cricket in the garden with my little boys. From my position at the wickets I could see right into the house through an open door, down a passage and through the hall as far as the front door. The kitchen door opened into the passage. I distinctly saw the same face peeping round at me out of the kitchen door. I again only saw the upper half of the figure. I threw down the bat and ran in. No one was in the kitchen. One servant was out and I found that the other was up in her bedroom. . . . A little later in the year about 8 o'clock one evening, I was coming downstairs alone, when I heard a voice from the direction, apparently, of my little boys' bedroom, the door of which was open. It distinctly said, in a deep, sorrowful tone, 'I can't find it.' I called out to my little boys, but they did not reply, and I have not the slightest doubt that they were asleep; they always called out if they heard me upstairs. My step-daughter, who was downstairs in the dining-room, with the door open, also heard the voice, and, thinking it was me calling, cried out, 'What are you looking for?' We were extremely puzzled. The voice could not by any possibility have belonged to any member of the household. The servants were in the kitchen and my husband was out. A short time after I was again coming downstairs after dark in the evening, when I felt a sharp slap on the back. It startled but did not hurt me. There was no one near me and I ran downstairs and told my husband and my step-daughter." The step-daughter had similar experiences, and the face she saw was the same as that seen by her step-mother. Once when playing with her brother on the landing, she happened to look back over her shoulder and saw the face again. Her brother at the same moment said, "There's a man on the landing."

This is a typical example of the haunting ghost, except that on one occasion this ghost spoke, which is a very rare thing for a ghost to do. Ghosts pay less attention to the inhabitants of the houses in which they appear than do crisis-apparitions, but they do pay *some* attention, witness the slap on the back, and the description of the face as "peeping round at me out of the kitchen door."

It will be seen how great is the similarity between the four classes of apparitions. The figures *look like* living human beings but *behave* in a somnambulistic manner; and ghosts are more somnambulistic than other classes of apparition, and seem to be less informed by a definite purpose.

These two characteristics of apparitions, their life-like resemblance to human beings on the one hand, and their somnambulistic or automatic behaviour on the other, present an incongruity. Since the dawn of history ghosts have been known and have manifested these two contradictory attributes; and I believe that this is the reason for the existence of beliefs concerning a future life which have been current since the earliest times. The first characteristic, the life-like resemblance to human beings, led to the apparition being identified with a human being in a naïve and literal way. Yet, at the same time, the intangible, evanescent, and tenuous nature of the apparition led to its being regarded as a "spirit." (Note that the term "spirit" is also used for evanescent liquids—liquids which quickly evaporate and disappear.) But if an apparition *is*, literally, a human being, and at the same time is something immaterial, it must be the immaterial part of a human being. Thus "spirit" came to mean the immaterial self, or essence of selfhood, *as well as* an apparition. The second characteristic of apparitions, their semi-conscious or automatic behaviour, led to the quite incompatible view that they were mere empty simulacra or "shades." The two beliefs together thus gave rise to the idea, so prevalent in antiquity, that the dead become ghosts who, in losing the body, lose their hold on real life, and wander in a state of semi-consciousness through a gloomy underworld. One finds it told in classical literature how the shade of a departed hero must first drink of the blood of the sacrifice in order to regain sufficient strength to speak and remember.

Myers, in one place, quotes the following apt passage from Homer. "There is some soul or wraith even in Hades, but there is no *heart* in them." No *heart* in them! This surely sums up the character not only of ghosts but of many of the manifestations we meet with in psychical research. Apparitions are wavering, uncertain, semi-intelligent things, and the majority of people still regard it as ludicrous to spend time in examining them, while science thrusts them aside as empty stories. It is to the credit of psychical research (and perhaps this constitutes one of the main differences between psychical research and Spiritualism) to have recognized that these evanescent manifestations, however unsatisfactory on the surface, are psychological phenomena which, if understood, would afford a deep insight into the recesses of personality. Moreover, these apparitions, which "have no heart in them," reappear in other forms. I mean that when we come to deal with trance and automatic writing we meet with similar entities, but now expressed in verbal instead of in sensory form. These two offer us a challenge, and, if examined, will tell us a great deal about the nature of the human being. The important thing for us is to get away from the ancient and literal view which takes these things at their face value and to probe beneath the surface. Myers goes on to say that, in Homer's view, it was the dead men *themselves* who were lying on the plain of Troy; and it took the mysticism of Plotinus to say, "The shade of Herakles might boast thus to shades; but the true Herakles for all this cares nought; being transported into a more sacred place, and strenuously engaging, even above his strength, in those contests in which the wise wish to engage." There is much behind these psychical appearances.

It is, perhaps, worth while to notice how true the ghost has always been to its character. The following account comes from Graeco-Roman times. "Cicero had said that faith in immortality was sustained by the fact of spirits returning to the world of sense. In the first and second centuries there was no lack of such aids to faith. Apparitions became the commonest facts of life and only the hardiest minds remained incredulous. . . . Eucrates has seen such spirits a thousand times, and, from long habit, has lost all fear of them. . . . As he lay in bed reading the *Phaedo,* his 'sainted wife,' who had recently died, appeared to him and reproached him because, among all the finery which had been burnt upon her pyre, a single gold-spangled shoe, which had slipped under the wardrobe, had been forgotten. Plutarch reports, apparently with perfect faith, the appearance of such spectral visitors at Chaeronea. The younger Pliny consulted his friend Sura as to the reality of such apparitions and reveals his faith in the gruesome tale of a haunted house at Corinth, where a restless ghost, who had often disturbed the quiet of the night with the clank of chains, was tracked to the mystery of a hidden grave."[11]

It has been pointed out that ghosts differ from crisis-apparitions in that they haunt places instead of appearing to people; and there has been a tendency in consequence to regard them as entirely different phenomena. But a study of the evidence shows that there is not, in fact, this radical difference; for crisis-apparitions move about in the physical

[11] Samuel Dill, *Roman Society from Nero to Marcus Aurelius,* p. 490.

surroundings of the percipient during their short appearances and may be said, in a sense, to "haunt" these surroundings in much the same way that ghosts do. Single visitations cannot, of course, properly be called "haunting"; but the point is that the crisis-apparition, when it appears in physical space, becomes a spatio-temporal phenomenon of exactly the same kind as the ghost. The difference between ghosts and crisis-apparitions is not that they are intrinsically different, but that they are inspired by two different *themes*. When we come to examine the characteristics of apparitions in greater detail, we shall see to how great an extent all four classes fall under the same specification. It is, of course, possible that there may be apparitions of quite a different kind from those which form the bulk of collection made by the Society for Psychical Research. I am not concerned to deny this possibility, but only to say that if there are, they lie outside the scope of the present survey.

The early workers in the subject were interested chiefly in the theory of the first two classes, namely experimental and crisis-apparitions. It had been previously supposed that if anyone saw an apparition, and especially if more than one person saw it at a time, that was proof of the presence of something physically objective. Myers and Gurney made the great advance of challenging this view and of regarding the apparition as a telepathic phenomenon. But so deeply ingrained is the habit of literal realism that even to-day, after the telepathic explanation has been before the world for more than half a century, people still believe that if they admit the existence of apparitions at all, they must regard them as "spirits."

Let us now look at the theories put forward by Gurney and Myers.

## 6. THEORIES HELD BY GURNEY AND MYERS

Myers in 1888 put forward the theory that apparitions, or phantasms of the living as well as of the dead, are telepathic phenomena. According to this theory the agent, while undergoing some crisis, which might or might not be death, sent a telepathic message to the percipient who embodied the message in sensory form, and this constituted the apparition. This theory in its general outline has, I think, been accepted by those acquainted with psychical research ever since, although Myers himself was not consistent about it and held quite a different theory with regard to one part of the evidence. I suggest, however, that the theory is correct as far as it goes, only that it leaves a great deal unsaid.

The chief difficulty which arose concerning this telepathic theory was that a very fair number of apparitional cases, both visual and auditory, were perceived collectively. There are too many well evidenced collective cases for any reasonable doubt to exist on this point. It might not be surprising if the agent, at the moment of his crisis, were to send a telepathic message to two or three of his friends at once, wherever they happened to be. But that is not what happens in collective cases. Such a telepathic message appears to be sent to one such friend and he sees the apparition. But this same apparition is seen by anyone else standing near who happens to be sufficiently sensitive, whoever he may be. And occasionally a bystander sees the apparition while the person principally interested does not. In fact, while it seems to be true that the condition for perceiving a telepathic apparition in the first instance is that of standing in a relation of interest or sympathy to the agent, the condition for *sharing* this experience is merely that of being in the physical neighbourhood of the primary percipient. This creates a peculiar difficulty for the telepathic theory of apparitions; but, as we shall see when we look more deeply into the characteristics of apparitions, the same difficulty is raised by other features as well. To see an apparition while in the waking state is a very rare experience, and Gurney realized that the probability that two or more people would have this experience at exactly the same time and in exactly the same place, unless both experiences were directly caused by the agent, is infinitesimal.

## 7. GURNEY'S THEORY

Gurney recognized three possibilities for explaining collective apparitions: (i) that the phantom is physically present in space where it is seen, (ii) that an agent, A, telepathically influences percipients B and C, etc., each independently, and that each percipient responds by creating his own sensory image, (iii) that an agent, A, telepathically influences, in the first place, the primary percipient B, in whom he is interested, and that B, while creating his own sensory image, acts as an agent, in turn transmitting the apparition on to C, who repeats the process, retransmitting the apparition to D, and so on. Gurney himself describes the process as a spreading by "infection."

Both Gurney and Myers agreed in rejecting the first theory of physical presence, for which course, indeed, there is ample evidence. The second is put out of court by considerations of improbability. And this improbability is still further increased by another consideration. Many crisis-apparitions occur just *after* the death of the agent and are supposed by Gurney to have been delayed in emergence by the percipient. In collective cases, therefore, the period of delay must be so exactly the same with the different percipients that all see the apparition at precisely the same moment, a most unlikely thing to happen. Gurney is therefore left with the third explanation, which he adopts, though not, I think, with any great enthusiasm.

Myers raised an objection to this third explanation by pointing out that there is no independent evidence that hallucinations tend to spread by "infection"; that, so far as purely subjective hallucinations are concerned, they never appear to do so. Gurney thereupon modified his theory to meet this by supposing that the telepathic influence of the agent, A, acts not only *on* the primary percipient, B, but also, in some way, *through* him, thus speeding the hallucination on its way to C and D, etc. He further suggested that when people are together in the same place, their minds are occupied to a large extent with similar topics and that this might account for the importance of physical proximity in selecting those to whom the apparition was to spread. Gurney, however, gives the impression that he offers this theory, not because he is entirely satisfied with it, but because it is the best he can suggest.

It is worth while at this point to consider for a moment the theory of telepathic deferment by which Gurney brought apparitions occurring directly after death into the category of "phantasms of the living." Any recognized crisis-apparitions seen within 12 hours after the death of the agent were supposed to have been received by the agent at or before the moment of death and to have been delayed in emergence. The 12-hour limit is arbitrary, being taken as the maximum time it is reasonable to allow for deferment; and for statistical purposes, an apparition seen within the period of 12 hours before to 12 hours after the death is considered as "coinciding" with the death. The chief evidence on which the theory of deferment is based is derived from some experiments in the telepathic transference of tastes.[12] In a few cases the percipient did not experience the taste until some minutes after the agent had finished tasting the substance. There were also some experiments which Mr. and Mrs. Newnham carried out with planchette in which replies to questions emerged only gradually.[13] It seems rather a long step from these to the crisis-deferments; but there may now be better evidence for deferment. Deferred hallucinations are easily produced in hypnosis, but there the idea of the delay is part of the *content* of the suggested idea. For a crisis-case to be parallel to this, the agent would have to *wish* the percipient to see his apparition at some later time. I have no doubt that under these circumstances the delay would occur. But in most crisis-cases there is no evidence of this designed delay; there is, on the contrary, a great deal of urgency.

The reason given for the supposed deferment is that the percipient is so engrossed with the business of life when the telepathic influence reaches him that it has no chance to emerge until he goes to bed or until some period of quiet supervenes. But if we study the evidence we shall see that there are many cases in which apparitions are seen while percipients are up and about their ordinary business. Indeed, the impression given is that the apparition often breaks in almost with violence. It may be worth while to quote a case in which the apparition occurred some time after the agent's crisis (more than 12 hours), but in which the delay was evidently not due to the fact that it was waiting for a quiet moment in which to emerge.

[12] *P.L.* I. p. 56.     [13] *P.L.* I. pp. 63-71.

An employer had befriended a youth called Robert Mackenzie, who had conceived in return a great veneration for him. One night his employer had a dream, which was more than a dream, for it was so realistic that in the narrative he says, "I cannot call it a dream." In this vision or apparition, Robert Mackenzie appeared advancing diffidently towards his employer, who was engaged in his office, and said that he must speak to him urgently. He asked forgiveness for a thing which he was accused of doing, but which, he said, he had never done. A peculiar feature of the apparition was the "bluish-pale" colour of the face and certain vivid spots on the forehead. This pseudo-dream or impression occurred on Tuesday morning just before 8 a.m. Immediately after it, news arrived by post that Robert Mackenzie had committed suicide by drinking nitric acid during the workmen's ball on the previous Saturday evening, and that he had died on Sunday. Afterwards, however, it came to be realized that it was not a case of suicide, but that Mackenzie had drunk the nitric acid in mistake for whisky. The appearance of the face was veridical and reproduced the symptoms of nitric acid poisoning.[14]

Gurney, presumably, would not advance his deferment theory to cover this case because the 12-hour period was exceeded. But clearly it is idle to suggest that it was a purely subjective hallucination reproducing these veridical details by chance. If we apply the deferment theory we find that the usual reason given for deferment does not apply; for if the percipient received the telepathic impulse from Robert Mackenzie on the Sunday when he died, but was too busy for it to be able to emerge, why did it not emerge when he went to bed on Sunday night instead of waiting till Tuesday morning?

## 8. MYER'S THEORY

Myers was sufficiently impressed by the difficulties confronting Gurney's theory to hold a different one himself, so far as collective hallucinations were concerned. Though he agreed with Gurney that apparitions are not *physical* phe-

[14] *Proc.* iii. 95-8.

nomena, he held that they do, at any rate in collective cases, in some real way, occupy space. "I hold," he says, "that when the phantasm is discerned by more than one person at once (and on some other but not all other occasions) it is actually effecting a change in that portion of space where it is perceived, although not, as a rule, in the matter which occupies that place. It is, therefore, not optically or acoustically perceived; perhaps no rays of light are reflected nor waves of air set in motion; but an unknown form of supernormal perception, not necessarily acting through sensory end-organs, comes into play."[15] It will be seen that there is in Myers's theory a note of uncertainty as to what actually happens. He speaks in another place of "actual spatial changes induced in the metetherial, but not in the material world." So that he would seem to regard space as something which enters into the "metetherial" as well as into the material order, though matter does not. He tends to halt between two opinions, Gurney's on the one hand and his own on the other. The "special idiosyncrasy on the part of the agent which tends to make his phantom easily visible" he calls "psychorrhagic diathesis," a term indicating the breaking loose of the soul. That which breaks loose is not, he thinks, "the whole vital principle of the organism" but a "psychical element probably of very varying character, and definable mainly by its power of producing a phantasm, perceptible by one or more persons, in some portion or other of space." He continues, "I hold that this phantasmogenetic effect may be produced either on the mind, and consequently on the brain of another person— in which case he may discern the phantasm somewhere in his vicinity, according to his own mental habit or prepossession—or else directly on a portion of space, 'out in the open,' in which case several persons may simultaneously discern the phantasm in that actual spot."[16]

According to this, Myers seems to have held something akin to Gurney's theory for cases of single percipience but to have held a theory of psychical, but not physical, invasion of space to account for collective cases. Myers never made it very clear what, exactly, he meant by "metetherial." He says that, "the world where life and thought are carried on apart from

15 *H.P.* II. p. 75.          16 *H.P.* I. p. 264.

matter, must certainly rank again as a new, a *metetherial* environment. In giving it this name I expressly imply only that from our human point of view it lies after or beyond the ether, as metaphysics lies after or beyond physics."[17] We must make what we can of that: but it is fairly clear that if he was right in supposing that some conscious or semi-conscious element of the agent's personality is present in space where the apparition is collectively seen, this is incompatible with Gurney's theory of telepathic deferment in post-mortem cases. For Myers's theory, all recognized post-mortem cases, collectively perceived, whether falling within the 12-hour limit or not, must definitely imply some sort of survival.

Myers's "spatial invasion" theory has the merit of overcoming the most serious objection to Gurney's theory, namely, the objection that in collective cases percipients not only see *some* apparition all at the same time, but that all see what in ordinary language we should call the *same* apparition. Gurney appears to think that there is insufficient evidence to show that they do all see the same apparition; but I cannot agree with him (see below, Ch. II, §5). Moreover, difficulties of just as formidable kind as those from which Gurney tries to escape by means of his theory of "infectious" telepathic spreading from one percipient to another arise in cases where there is only one percipient (see Chapter II). If Gurney's explanation were true, we might expect that all the percipients in a collective case would see figures having a rough resemblance to one another or, at any rate, figures which were connected with a single theme; but they could not possibly be expected to see exactly correlated aspects of the same figure. Nor should we expect the temporal synchronism to be exact. We should expect the same sort of agreement which we sometimes get in telepathic experiments when the target is, say, a factory chimney and one percipient gets a pyramid and another a telegraph pole. What we find in the collective percipience of apparitions, and not only in the collective percipience but in the single percipience also, is a miraculously accurate copy of what happens in normal sense-perception. Gurney seems to have felt the difficulty, but felt driven to adopt the less difficult of what he con-

[17] *H.P.* I. pp. 215-16.

sidered to be the only two plausible theories. "I feel absolutely driven," he says, "to suppose that where C's experience resembles B's, it is *in some direct way* connected with B's; this is the only alternative that I can see to admitting a physical basis to the percept."[18]

If Myers's explanation of an invasion of physical space be accepted for collective cases, there seems no valid reason for not adopting it in all cases. But I find it impossible to separate Myers's theory from the theory of a physical apparition, and I agree with Gurney in rejecting it. Space is, after all, a conception which cannot be separated from the perceived properties of physical objects, and I cannot see how a distinction can be drawn between physical and non-physical ("metetherial") occupation of space; nor, indeed, that non-physical occupation of space means anything. Perhaps it may be thought that this question can be put to the test by appealing to the evidence. It might be said that if there is evidence to show that an apparition is aware of viewing a scene from some particular standpoint in space, that is proof that its consciousness occupied that position. There is undoubtedly evidence to show that apparitions behave *as if* they were aware of their surroundings and therefore of being at a particular place among them; but behaving *as if* aware is not the same thing as *being* aware, or we could say that the figures on the cinematograph screen were consciously aware of being there. I am prepared, however, to admit more than this. There is a small amount of evidence that the apparition of a living person can be seen at a place in space and that the person afterwards remembers viewing the scene from that identical position. (See Ch. IV, §1, Case 36.) There are also the cases of "travelling clairvoyance," quoted in Chapter IV, in which the sensitive describes a distant scene as from a particular point of view. But, perverse as it may seem, I am not prepared to accept this as evidence that the conscious self of the sensitive actually *occupied* that spatial point of view. I carry my perverseness even further than that and refuse to admit that the conscious self of a person who is talking to me in the same room is present in that room, or, indeed, is anywhere in space.

[18] *P.L.* II. p. 266.

Meanwhile, I venture to think that Gurney and Myers did not exhaust the possible theories of apparitions, though they laid the foundations on which any valid explanation of apparitions must be based. Since their day the theory of normal sense-perception has been more thoroughly worked out, and it is by the aid of this theory that I believe the true solution is to be found. Before going into this matter it will, however, be advisable to examine the evidence with greater care and to collect all the information we can about the nature of apparitions.

# Chapter II

## Characteristics of Apparitions

THE FOUR CLASSES of apparitions, as has been said, comprise, (1) Experimental Cases, (2) Crisis-cases, (3) Post-mortem Cases, and (4) Ghosts. Cutting across these cases, as it were at right angles, are a number of characteristics common in a greater or lesser degree to all the classes. These characteristics are very instructive and each is illustrated below by a few examples, given in abbreviated form; while references to further examples are given in the footnotes. These examples together do not, of course, exhaust the evidence for the characteristics, and the student will have no difficulty in finding more.

### 1. SPATIAL PRESENTATION

The first characteristic to be noticed is that visual apparitions appear in different kinds of space. O course visual dreams occur in a space of their own which has nothing to do with the space of the waking world. But waking hallucinations, with which we are now particularly concerned, also adopt various types of spatial presentation, which are best described by means of examples.

CASE 7 A Mr. F. Gottschalk had written to a friend of his, who was to give a recitation at the Prince's Theatre, to ask at what time it would be. "In the evening," he says, "I was going out to see some friends, when on the road there seemed suddenly to develop itself before me a disc of light, which appeared to be on a different plane to everything else in view. It was not possible for me to fix the distance at which it seemed to be from me. Examining the illuminated space, I found that two hands were visible. They were engaged in drawing a letter from an envelope which I instinctively felt to be mine and in consequence thought immediately that the hands were those of Mr. Thorpe. . . . I examined the picture, and found that the hands were very white, and bared up to some distance above the wrist. Each forearm terminated in a ruffle; beyond that nothing was to be seen." About that time, Mr. Gottschalk discovered afterwards, his friend had received his letter at the theatre. "The whiteness of the hands," he says, "was accounted for by the fact that actors invariably whiten their hands when playing a part like the one Mr. Thorpe was engaged in—'Snake' in 'The School for Scandal.' The ruffles also formed part of the dress for this piece."

Incidentally a M. Marillier, who gave an interesting account of some experiences of his in the *Revue Philosophique* for 1886, p. 212, endorses the indescribableness of this kind of appearance in space. "Je ne pourrais indiquer ni la place de l'image que j'ai objectivée, ni la distance à laquelle elle se trouve."

CASE 8 Another variation in the mode of spatial presentation is as follows. "I was sitting in the Birmingham Town Hall with my husband at a concert, when there came over me the icy chill which usually accompanies these occurrences. Almost immediately, I saw with perfect distinctness, between myself and the orchestra, my uncle, Mr. W., lying in bed with an appealing look on his face, like one dying. I had not heard anything of him for several months, and had no reason to think he was ill. The appearance was not transparent or filmy, but perfectly solid-looking; *and yet I could somehow see the orchestra, not through, but behind it.*" The percipient's uncle died at the time when she saw the vision.

CASE 9   Quite a different device was adopted in the following example. Dr. A. S. Wiltse describes an incident which occurred in Tennessee. He and his wife, together with their hosts, Mr. and Mrs. Todd, had retired to rest in the one-roomed house or cabin. "While we were talking," he says, "I saw a picture slide on to the wall at my feet, at such a height as to rest easily in my line of vision. I called to Mr. and Mrs. Todd to cease talking and told them what I saw. The picture was some feet in size each way and remained before me long enough for me to describe it in detail to them. It was a landscape, the main features in which were a river with a large creek emptying into it very nearly at right angles. When I had given a full description, the picture disappeared with a quick movement like that with which it had appeared, but in the opposite direction from which it came. Mr. Todd said, 'You have described Emerald River and Rock Creek where it empties into it.' " Three more pictures appeared and disappeared in similar fashion, giving in pictorial form a tragedy in which a man, shot by a gun, staggered out of a recognized house and fell dead. The tragedy actually happend some months afterwards.

CASE 10   Here, again, is another. "At Fiesole . . . I was giving my little children their dinner. . . . I had to stand . . . and give my attention to what I was doing—on raising my head . . . the wall opposite me seemed to open, and I saw my mother lying dead on her bed in her little house at—. Some flowers were at her side and on her breast; she looked calm but unmistakably dead, and the coffin was there. It was so real that I could scarcely believe that the wall was really brick and mortar, and not a transparent window." She found that her mother had died in England six days before.

CASE 11   The following is a very curious presentational device. About six weeks after the death of a certain Captain Towns at his residence near Sydney in Australia, the narrator's wife entered one of the rooms about 9 p.m., together with a Miss Berthon. The gas was burning. "They were amazed to see, reflected as it were on the polished surface of the wardrobe, the image of Captain Towns. It was . . . like an ordinary medallion portrait, but lifesize. . . . Surprised and half alarmed at what they saw, their first idea was that a portrait had been hung in the room, and that what they saw was its reflection—but there was no picture of any kind. Whilst they were looking and wondering . . . Miss Towns came into the room, and before either of the others had time to speak she exclaimed, 'Good gracious! Do you see papa!' " One of the housemaids, happening to pass, was called in and said, "Oh, Miss! The master!" Captain Towns's old servant was sent for and exclaimed, "Oh, Lord save us! Mrs. Lett, it's the Captain!" The butler and nurse were called and saw the image. "Finally Mrs. Towns was sent for, and, seeing the apparition, she advanced towards it with her arm extended as if to touch it, and as she passed her hand over the panel of the wardrobe the figure gradually faded away, and never again appeared."

In all these cases the imagery is not of an inward type, such as might occur in vivid memory or imagination. It is *external* imagery, but occupying a special space of its own and not the space of material things.

CASE 12  In the next example, this is still the case, but the private space in which the scene appears is not of a pictorial kind. It is a reproduction of the space in which the event depicted occurred, and the percipient appears to be observing the scene from a point in that space.

Mrs. Paquet, whose brother was a stoker in a tug plying in Chicago harbour, awoke feeling gloomy and depressed and could not shake the feeling off. She went into the pantry and was about to make some tea, when, she says, "as I turned around my brother Edmund—or his exact image—stood before me and only a few feet away. The apparition stood with back toward me, or, rather, partially so, and was in the act of falling forward—away from me—seemingly impelled by two loops or a loop of rope drawing against his legs. The vision lasted but a moment, disappearing over a low railing or bulwark, but was very distinct. I dropped the tea, clasped my hands to my face, and exclaimed, 'My God! Ed is drowned.' " She noticed certain veridical details, particularly the legs of his pants, rolled up and showing their white lining. The tragedy had happened as she saw it about six hours earlier.

The case is curious. Mrs. Paquet is aware of *two* three-dimensional spaces at the same time (she mentions the figure as falling *away* from her); and she has a point of observation in each. In one she is in her pantry; in the other she is standing on the deck of the tug, and it is presumably from this latter standpoint that the figure appears to be "only a few feet away." She is therefore, for the short time during which the apparition lasts, perceptually conscious of being in two spaces *which bear no spatial relation to one another*. It is a point to note that perceived spaces, in which one is present as an observer, *can* be spatially unrelated to one another.

CASE 13  The percipient may appear to be simply in the space in which the crisis is occurring to the agent, without this bi-location. The writer of this narrative felt depressed and went to the nursery to amuse himself with the children. "The thought of Mr. M— came into my mind," he says, "and suddenly with my eyes open, as I believe, for I was not feeling sleepy, I seemed to be in a room in which a man was lying dead in a small bed. I recognized the face at once as that of Mr. M—, and felt no doubt that he was dead, and not asleep only. The room appeared to be bare and without carpet or furniture. . . . I tried to argue with myself that there could be nothing in what I had seen, chiefly on the ground that from what I knew of Mr. M—'s circumstances it was most improbable that, if dead, he would be in a room in so bare and unfurnished a state." Mr. M— had died suddenly on the day of the apparition in a small village hospital in a warm foreign climate.

Another and more striking example of this kind will be found in Case 36 (Ch. IV, §1).

The majority of visions, however, take place in common, visual space and move about among the percipient's material surroundings. Examples of these have been given in Cases 3-6. There is evidence that auditory as well as visual apparitions occur, as a rule, in physical space.

CASE 14  In the following auditory case, the percipient had been given a letter, which had been considerably delayed in transit, to forward to the addressee, who was known to her brother. Whilst waiting for her brother to return home, she put the letter on the mantelpiece. Presently she heard a sound of ticking coming from the mantelpiece and searched the

room in vain for a watch or clock which might account for
it. The ticking, which was loud and sharp, obviously came
from the letter, so she moved it to various parts of the room,
but it still continued ticking. After a while the sound got on
her nerves, and she sat in the hall till her brother returned.
When he entered the room she asked him if he heard anything
and he said, "I hear a watch or clock ticking." Then he went
to the letter and exclaimed, "Why, the letter is ticking." Together they moved it about and examined it, but it plainly
contained nothing but a sheet of paper. The brother took
the letter to the addressee, who found that it contained an
intimation of her husband's death.

But there are occasions on which an auditory hallucination
does not proceed from a definite point in space, but appears to
the percipient to be more like an inward voice.

It may be gathered from these cases that a telepathic hallucination can *choose* the particular form of its sensory expression; but as a general rule, if the percipient is awake, it
chooses to appear in ordinary space. Apparitions are thus
in no way bound to appear in the space in which material
things exist. They *can* appear in common space, but that is
only one out of several possible modes of appearance. There
is an unbroken transition from appearances in space, through
apearances in detached and private spaces, to appearances
in crystals, in dreams, or in inward types of vision. Apparitions, when they appear in space, are in no way more real or,
so to speak, more actually *there,* than they are when they
adopt any other mode of self-expression. Their exact similarity
to material things is *imitative.*

## 2. NON-PHYSICAL CHARACTER

The second characteristic of the classes of apparitions with
which we have to deal is that none of them are physical
phenomena. If, indeed, there are such things as physical apparitions, as the evidence for poltergeists would appear to
suggest, they lie outside my present terms of reference, and
in any case form a very small proportion of those collected
by the Society for Psychical Research.

The evidence for the non-physical character of apparitions

arises from the following circumstances: (i) they appear and disappear in locked rooms; (ii) they vanish while being watched; (iii) they sometimes become transparent and fade away; (iv) they are often seen and heard by some of those present but not by all; (v) they disappear into walls and closed doors and pass through physical objects; (vi) people have put their hands through them and walked through them without encountering any resistance; (vii) they leave no physical traces behind them.

CASE 15  For example, a landowner, on terms of acquaintance but not of friendship with his tenant, is asked by the latter to come in one evening and smoke a cigar with him. The landlord refuses, and, as they separate, the tenant exclaims, "Then, if you will not come, good-bye." The landlord, according to the story, says that he spent the evening in his dining-room and that it was a bright, clear night. He then adds, "Since I had come in slight snow had fallen, just sufficient to make the ground show white." He went into the breakfast-room later, and about 10 o'clock was standing just inside the shuttered window, studying a book by the light of the lamp. His shoulder, he adds, was touching the shutter. "I distinctly heard the front gate opened," he continues, "and shut again with a clap, and footsteps advancing at a run up the drive; when opposite the window the steps changed from sharp and distinct on the gravel to dull and less clear on the grass slip below the window, and at the same time I was conscious that someone or something stood close to me outside, only the thin shutter and a sheet of glass dividing us. I could hear the quick panting laboured breathing of the messenger, or whatever it was, as if trying to recover breath before speaking. . . . Suddenly, like a gunshot, inside, outside and all around, there broke out the most appalling shriek—a prolonged wail of horror, which seemed to freeze the blood. It was not a single shriek, but more prolonged, commencing in a high key, and then less and less, wailing away towards the north and becoming weaker and weaker as it receded on sobbing pulsations of intense agony. Of my fright and horror I can say nothing—increased tenfold when I walked into the dining-room and found my wife sitting quietly at her work close to the window, in the same line and distant only 10 to 12 feet from the corresponding window in the breakfast-room. *She had heard nothing."*

In the morning an examination of the ground under the window showed no footsteps in the snow, which was still there, either on the grass or in the drive.

About 10 o'clock that evening, the tenant had committed suicide by taking poison in his own house.

The evidence for the non-physical character of the occurrence is twofold: (a) the failure of the percipient's wife to hear the shriek, and (b) the absence of footmarks in the snow in places where footsteps had been heard.

CASE 16   The well-authenticated ghost, studied by Miss Morton, which was seen and heard by a number of people over a period of years, proved its non-physical character in many ways. Miss Morton fixed threads across the stairs, very lightly secured by pellets of marine glue, and twice watched the apparition pass through them without disturbing them. She was also frequently watching the apparition when it disappeared in its accustomed place near the garden door. Towards the end of its existence, it faded away gradually. "The figure became much less substantial," says Miss Morton, "on its later appearances. Up to about 1886 it was so solid and life-like that it was often mistaken for a real person. It gradually became less distinct. At all times it intercepted the light; we have not been able to ascertain if it cast a shadow." Miss Morton kept a camera handy in the hope of making an attempt to photograph the ghost, but never had a suitable opportunity.

Once, she reported, "while coming up the garden, I walked towards the orchard, when I saw the figure cross the orchard, go along the carriage drive in front of the house, and in at the open side door, across the hall and into the drawing-room, I following. She crossed the drawing-room, and took up her usual position behind the couch in the bow window. My father came in soon after, and I told him she was there. He could not see the figure, but went up to where I showed him she was. She then went swiftly round behind him, across the room, out of the door and along the hall, disappearing as usual near the garden door, we both following her." The figure cannot have been physical, since Miss Morton saw it while her father did not.

Often the footsteps of the figure were heard by various members of the household without any figure being seen. On one occasion five people, standing on either side of the passage, heard the footsteps going up and down the passage between them: but although they felt a cold breeze (which, however, did not blow their candle-flames about), they saw nothing. This again is proof of the non-physical nature of the sounds, for a figure whose feet were so unsubstantial as not to reflect light-waves could scarcely create physical sound-waves by bringing its feet into contact with the floor.

CASE 17  In some cases the apparition enters the room by the door, and the door is seen, and sometimes also heard, to open and close. But the physical door is closed, and in some instances locked, all the while. The door which is seen to open and close is thus not a physical door.

Two boys, aged 19 and 23, sons of a chemist at Leominster, give an account of twice seeing the same figure come into their bedroom. Speaking of the second visit, the narrator says, "The bedroom door was shut all night on this occasion, and I was lying awake when I saw the door open and someone peep round. I thought it was one of our assistants come for a lark to pull me out of bed . . . however, I lay still, and then the door seemed to open wide, so I leaned out of bed to give it a hard push and everything vanished, and I nearly fell out of bed, for the door was shut as when I went to bed." This is direct evidence of the unsubstantial nature of the apparitional door.

CASE 18  The following case again illustrates the non-physical character of apparitional sounds. "I was sitting with my mother in 8 Suffolk Place, Pall Mall East," says the percipient. "The house was empty except for ourselves. The room was mainly lighted by a large skylight. The house was quite quiet. . . . Suddenly we were both startled by a terrifying noise, as if a cartload of gravel had been shot down from a height on to the skylight. I jumped up in startled alarm, thinking that the skylight was, of course, smashed to pieces by the stones which I had actually heard falling on it. There was not the slightest trace of anything unusual. My mother, who had had many warnings of different kinds, was less alarmed. She took it for granted that someone was dead. . . ." A relation of whom they were fond had died at the time. The sounds must have been hallucinatory.

CASE 19  Gurney quotes a case which he does not allow as evidence for telepathy, but which is nevertheless instructive as evidence for the character of apparitions. It must be remembered that we are now dealing with the character of hallucinatory percepts, and it is only of secondary importance whether the cases quoted are really telepathic or not. The narrator and his niece were sitting in the drawing-room about 2 p.m. "I saw what I supposed at the first moment to be dirty soapy water running in at the door; and I was in the act of jumping up to scold the housemaid for upsetting the water, when I saw that the supposed water was the tail or train of a lady's dress. The lady glided in backwards, as if she had been slid in on a slide, each part of her dress keeping its place without disturbance. She glided in till I could see the whole of her, *except the tip of her nose, her lips and the tip of her chin, which were hidden by the edge of the door*. Her head was slightly turned over her shoulder, and her eyes also turned, so that it appeared fixed upon me. She held her arm, which was a very fine one, in a peculiar way, as if she were proud of it. She was dressed in a pale blue evening dress, worked with white lace. I instantly recognized the figure as a lady whom I had known some 25 years or more before; and with whom I had frequently danced. She was a bright, dashing girl, a good dancer, and we were good friends, but nothing more. She had afterwards married, and I had occasionally heard of her, but do not think I had seen her for certainly more than 20 or 25 years. She looked much as I used to see her—with long curls and bright eyes, but perhaps something stouter and more matronly. I said to myself, 'This is one of those strange apparitions I have often heard of. I will watch it as carefully as I can.' My niece, who did not see the figure, in the course of a minute or two exclaimed, 'Uncle A., what is the matter with you? You look as if you saw a ghost!' I motioned her to be quiet; as I wished to observe the thing carefully; and an impression came upon me that if I moved, the thing would disappear. I tried to find out whether there was anything in the ornaments on the walls, or anything else which could suggest the figure: but I found all the lines close to her cut the outline of her figure at all sorts of angles, and none of these coincided with the outline of her figure, and the colour of everything around her strongly contrasted with her colour. In the course of a few minutes, I heard the door-bell ring, and I heard my brother's voice in the hall. He came upstairs, and walked right through the figure into the room. The figure then began to fade rather quickly, at first losing the colours and then the form. . . ."

Some years afterwards the percipient found that the lady had died, about seven months after the apparition, of cancer in the face. "She never showed me the front of her face," he says; "it was always concealed by the edge of the door."

The non-physical character of the figure is proved by the fact that his niece did not see it and his brother walked through it. In some ways the case is reminiscent of the subjective visions of Mr. A in Case 35 (p. 108).

Apparitions, then, combine two qualities. They are (a) nonphysical in character, yet, when at their best, they are (b) indistinguishable from material figures normally perceived, so far as the visual and auditory senses are concerned.

How is it with the sense of touch? It is not uncommon for the sense of touch to be hallucinated in apparitional cases. I have come across 56 cases of it, and no doubt there are more. The following are a few relevant sentences quoted from some of these cases. "I heard distinctly the footsteps of the gentleman to whom I was engaged, quickly mounting the stairs after me, and then I as plainly felt him put his arms round my waist."[1] "She was awakened by feeling a heavy weight on her feet, and on sitting up, saw the form of her husband seated on the bed."[2] ". . . he was suddenly aroused by feeling each of his hands firmly grasped and pressed. He instantly sat up, and by the bedside stood George, holding his hands and smiling in his face. . . ."[3] "Some one has taken hold of my hand; the hand was quite cold. I believe it was my aunt; I saw her rush out of the room."[4] ". . . of a sudden some one touched my shoulder with such force that I immediately

[1] *P.L.* (35).       [3] *P.L.* (179).
[2] *P.L.* (176).      [4] *P.L.* (180).

turned. You were there as plainly to be seen as if in the body. . . ."[5] ". . . a hand was placed on his shoulder, and a voice said distinctly: 'Joe, your mother wants you.' "[6] In one case the percipient heard her name called three times, and answered, thinking it was her uncle. The third time she recognized the voice of her mother, who had been dead 16 years. "I said, 'Mamma!' She then came round the screen near my bedside with two children in her arms, and placed them in my arms and put the bedclothes over them, and said, 'Lucy, promise to take care of them, for their mother is just dead.' . . . I remained, feeling the children to be still in my arms, and fell asleep. When I awoke there was nothing."[7] "I distinctly felt a pressure and a rustling of a dress at my side as if a woman had brushed past me."[8] "I was again coming downstairs after dark in the evening when I felt a sharp slap on the back. . . . There was no one near me."[9], and so on.

In nearly all cases it is the apparition which touches the percipient, and not the percipient who touches the apparition. The situation with regard to touch is curious. Touch, of course, is reciprocal; if the apparition is touching the percipient, the percipient is, at the same time, touching the apparition. But when a percipient tries actively to touch an apparition, he usually fails. In the case of the Morton ghost (Case 16), Miss Morton made several attempts to corner the figure and take hold of it, but it cleverly evaded her. "I also attempted to touch her," she says, "but she always eluded me. It was not that there was nothing to touch, but that she always seemed *beyond* me, and if followed into a corner, simply disappeared." Again, "I also tried especially to *touch* her, but did not succeed. On cornering her, as I did once or twice, she disappeared." This is interesting. It looks as if the reason for the failure to touch her was not because the figure was so quick in getting away, but because the boundary of the visual solid forming the figure was created always just beyond the reach of Miss Morton's hand, thus affording another proof of the subjective character of the apparition.

In only one case have I found that a percipient was successful in taking hold of a ghost.

[5] *P.L.* (569).     [7] *Proc.* x. 380.     [9] *Proc.* iii. 102.
[6] *P.L.* (293).     [8] *Proc.* iii. 89.

CASE 20   Two ladies were staying with a German family at Cassel, and were sleeping in a room supposed to be haunted by a knight. They both saw an apparition, and, the narrator says, "as soon as it came close to my bed, I seized it, and seemed to take hold of something soft, like flimsy drapery, but whatever it was seemed dragged from me by some invisible power. . . ."

It must be admitted that not many percipients have tried to take hold of apparitions. Too often, when the chance presented itself, they took refuge under the bedclothes instead!

One can see, I think, the reason for this shyness on the part of apparitions to being touched. It is not because the sense of touch cannot be hallucinated. Clearly it can be. It is because, if they allowed themselves to be touched, an anomalous situation would arise. Had Miss Morton, for example, felt the contour of her ghost by tactual hallucination and felt its body resistant and impenetrable, she would, while *feeling* her hand arrested by it, have *seen* her hand passing through it unimpeded; for there would be no visual hallucination so far as her own hand was concerned. The constructor of hallucinations, which appears to strive after consistency, evidently prefers to avoid such self-contradictory situations.

The evidence for the non-physical character of apparitions is overwhelming. I repeat that there may, for all I know, be physical apparitions *as well*. On that point I express no opinion; but if there are, they are phenomena of a totally different kind from the apparitions we are here dealing with.

### 3.  IMITATION OF NORMAL PERCEPTION

The third characteristic of apparitions is their remarkable imitation of normal perception. At first sight this may not strike the reader as strange; but it affords a most valuable clue to the nature of apparitions and to what- lies behind them. As far as it can, an apparition appears to aim at behaving exactly as a living human being would behave under the attendant circumstances. I shall instance five ways in which it does this.

(1) Apparitions *behave* as if they were aware of their surroundings. When one comes to think of it, nearly every

apparition which appears in physical space gives evidence of being aware of its surroundings. It may come in at the door. It nearly always moves about a room with normal respect for the position of the furniture. If it wanders about the house it makes normal use of doors, passages, and staircases. When Miss Morton's father went and stood by the figure, she reports that it "went swiftly round behind him," that is to say, it acted in response to his presence. (See Case 16.) Again, Miss Morton on more than one occasion spoke to the apparition. "I spoke to her as she passed the foot of the stairs," she says, "but she did not answer, although, as before, she stopped and seemed as though *about* to speak." Crisis-apparitions also frequently approach the percipient, look him in the face, speak to him, and even put a hand on his shoulder, thus giving evidence of what, in the case of a living person, we should take to be conscious appreciation of their surroundings and situation. It seems scarcely necessary to illustrate this with examples, but a typical one will be found in *Phantasms of the Living,* vol. i, p. 453, in which the apparition may almost be said to have crashed into the room, highly excited, and apparently well aware of what it was trying to do.

(2) Visible apparitions behave as a rule (there are some exceptions) with regard to the lighting of the scene, the distance from the percipient, and the presence of intervening objects, exactly as a material person would do. This, again, may not seem surprising at first sight; but it is very significant in view of the fact that the apparition has no physical basis, and no need to pay any attention to physical lighting.

CASE 21 Several narratives bring out this point. Here is one. "One moonlight night I was sleeping in my room . . . when I was awakened by hearing a noise close to my head, like the clinking of money. My waking idea, therefore, was that a *man* was trying to take my money out of my trousers pocket, which lay on a chair close to the head of my bed. On opening my eyes I was astonished to see a *woman,* and I well remember thinking with sorrow that it must be one of our servants who was trying to take my money. . . . When my eyes had become more accustomed to the light, I was more than ever surprised to see that it was my *mother,* dressed in a peculiar silver-grey dress, which she had originally got for a fancy-dress ball. She was standing with both hands stretched out in front of her as if feeling her way; and in that manner moved slowly away from me, passing in front of the dressing-table, which stood in front of the curtained window, through which the moon threw a certain amount of light. Of course my idea all this time was that she was walking in her sleep. On getting beyond the table she was lost to my sight in the darkness. I then sat up in bed, listening, but hearing nothing, and, on peering through the darkness, saw that the door, which was at the foot of my bed, and to get to which she would have to pass in front of the light, was still shut. I then jumped out of bed, struck a light, and instead of finding my mother at the far end of the room, as I expected, found the room empty." The present point is that the apparition was lost to his sight in the darkness.

Another illustration occurs in Case 5. The relevant sentence is, "As it [the apparition] passed the lamp, a deep shadow fell upon the room as of a material person shutting out the light from us by his intervening body, and he disappeared, as it were, into the wall."

Once more to quote the Morton ghost (Case 16). On the first occasion of her encountering the ghost Miss Morton says, "On opening the door I saw no one; but on going a few steps along the passage, I saw the figure of a tall lady, dressed in black, standing at the head of the stairs. After a few moments she descended the stairs, and I followed for a short distance, feeling curious what it could be. I had only a small piece of candle, and it suddenly burnt itself out; and being unable to see more, I went back to my room." When the candle burnt itself out, she could no longer see the apparition! That is the important point. In all these cases, and in the greater number of visual apparitions, the figure varies in visibility according to the physical lighting. But sometimes it is visible in the dark, seeming to shine with a light of its own.[10] It *need* not become invisible in the dark, but it usually does so because it is *trying to behave as much like a normally perceived figure as possible.*

For the same reason it obeys all the pysical laws of dis-

[10] See *Proc.* xxxiii. 367; *P.L.* II. p. 478; *Proc.* v. 450, etc.

tance and perspective on the majority of occasions. *But here again we can find exceptions.* One occurs in Case 32. The percipient, with two others, sees her father on horseback waving his hat. "As my father waved his hat," she says, "I clearly saw the Lincoln and Bennett mark inside, though from the distance we were apart it ought to have been utterly impossible for me to have seen it."

CASE 22 Lady Troubridge recounts how she and Miss Radclyffe-Hall had agreed to meet a friend at a garage to inspect a car. When approaching the garage she appeared to see her friend pointing to a car and gesticulating and recognized familiar details of her dress, the distance being about thirty feet. But her friend was not to be found in the garage and arrived ten minutes later, dressed as Lady Troubridge had seen her. "I not only saw her with normal distinctness," says the narrator, "but in a way too detailed in my opinion to be possible for normal vision at some 30 feet away. [Lady Troubridge remarks that she is very short-sighted.] . . . When I described what I had seen to Miss Radclyffe-Hall . . . I realized that I had noticed details in a manner which I thought, and still think, exceeded my normal visual powers at a distance." The amount of detail visible in an apparition, then, usually varies with distance as it would do in normal perception. *But it need not do so.*

(3) Consistently with the same principle, if the percipient shuts or screens his eyes, the apparition disappears. In normal vision, of course, the object we are looking at disappears when we shut our eyes because the light from it can no longer enter them. But in the case of an apparition, which is nonphysical, no light is reaching our eyes from it in any case, so that the shutting of them cannot make any difference to the process of our seeing it. I will merely quote the relevant sentences from three cases illustrating this point, without describing the cases themselves.

CASE 23 "As I was kneeling I looked towards the opposite gallery, which was of dark wood. There I saw the half-figure of my sister; the head and arms outstretched above the boy, as if blessing him. For a moment I thought it was impossible, and closed my eyes for a few seconds. Opening them again,

I saw the same beautiful form, which almost immediately vanished."

CASE 24 "That night I awoke suddenly, and saw facing the window of my room, by my bedside, surrounded by a sort of phosphorescent mist, as it were, my brother kneeling. I tried to speak, but could not. I buried my head in the clothes, not at all afraid . . . but simply to collect my ideas. . . . I decided that it must be fancy, and the moonlight playing on a towel, or something out of place. But on looking up, there he was again, looking lovingly, imploringly, and sadly at me."

CASE 25 "About three weeks after her [the grandmother's] death I awoke one morning in October, and saw distinctly the well-known tall figure, the calm old face, the large dark eyes uplifted as usual to the face of the old clock. I closed my eyes for some seconds, and then slowly reopened them. She stood there still. A second time I closed my eyes, a second time reopened them. She was gone."

These are good examples of imitative action on the part of apparitions. There is no necessity for the apparition to disappear when the percipient shuts his eyes. Note that in Case 35 it does not disappear. It is made to disappear in these cases only in order to simulate ordinary perception.

(4) It is not likely often to happen that a mirror is so placed relatively to an apparition that the percipient would, in a case of normal perception, see the apparition reflected in it. I have, however, come across three cases in which apparitions have been seen reflected in mirrors.

CASE 26 Four Miss Du Canes, all sisters, were on their way to bed at night, and Miss Louisa Du Cane entered her bedroom accompanied by one of her sisters and crossed to the mantelpiece at the further side to find a box of matches. The two remaining sisters also entered the room and stopped about half-way across it. As they stood, the door through which they had entered was behind them and their two sisters at the mantelpiece were on their left front. A door communicating with their mother's room was on their right front. (A plan is given with the account.) "There was no light," says Miss Louisa Du Cane, "beyond that which glimmered through the Venetian blinds in each room. As I stood by the mantelpiece I was awe-struck by the sudden appearance of a figure gliding noiselessly towards me from the outer room. The appearance was that of a young man, of middle height, dressed in dark clothes, and wearing a peaked cap. His face was very pale, and his eyes downcast as though in deep thought. His mouth was shaded by a dark moustache. The face was slightly luminous, which enabled us to distinguish the features distinctly, although we were without a light of any kind at the time. The apparition glided onwards towards my sisters, who were standing inside the room, quite close to the outer door, and who had first caught sight of it reflected in the mirror. When within a few inches from them it vanished as suddenly as it had appeared. As the figure passed we distinctly felt a cold air which seemed to accompany it." It is evident from the diagram that the two sisters would have seen the figure reflected in the mirror before they saw it directly.

CASE 27   Lady B. and her daughter, Miss B., lived in a house in which strange sounds had been heard on various occasions. One night, when both ladies were sleeping in the same room, they "suddenly started up wide awake without any apparent cause, and saw a figure in a white garment which might have been a night-dress, with dark, curly hair. . . . The room was not quite dark, although there was no artificial light except from the gas lamp in the square. No fear or any physical sensation was experienced. The figure was standing in front of the fire-place, over which was a mirror. The position was such as to show the face in quarter profile and to intercept its own reflection from the mirror. It was a female figure, with hair down the back. The face, so far as shown, was clearly visible. The two ladies both sprang out of bed to the doors, which they found locked. On turning round again the figure had disappeared." This was Lady B.'s account. Miss B., in her statement, says that she "saw the back of the figure and its long dark hair, but not the face. The face was, however, clearly reflected in the mirror. . . ."

CASE 28   The apparition in the next case was of a living person, who, however, died a fortnight later. The percipient says, "I stood before the mirror doing my hair, when I suddenly saw him coming from behind, as if approaching on tip-toe. His hands were outstretched, and I had an impression that he would place them on my shoulders; I could even hear his last step, like the squeak of a boot, as he put his foot down. I turned in surprise, and faced him, consequently seeing him out of the glass and in the glass. As I turned I exclaimed, 'Is that you?' At least I felt that I said that, but as I spoke he vanished."

The point, of course, which makes these mirror-cases so interesting is that no light from the apparition is being reflected by the mirror. They reveal powers of calculation and adaptation of the apparition to the physical conditions which border on the miraculous.[11]

(5) A feature of apparitions which is still less likely to attract the attention of a casual observer is that they almost invariably occupy the centre of the normal visual field. It will perhaps have been noticed that if the percipient turns his head away, just as when he hides it under the bedclothes, he ceases to see the apparition. This appears so natural that it does not at first strike us that, since the normal processes of vision are not taking place, it is not necessary that this should happen. It, too, is an *imitative* dramatic feature, as the following example shows.

CASE 29    The narrator of this case was sitting at home in the evening awaiting the return of a party of friends from a concert. They were overdue, and he sat down to read a book and had become absorbed in it. "Suddenly," he says, "without a moment's warning, my whole being seemed aroused to the highest state of tension or aliveness, and I was aware, with an intenseness not easily imagined by those who have never experienced it, that another being or presence was not only in the room but close to me. I put my book down, and although my excitement was great, I felt quite collected and not conscious of any sense of fear. Without changing my position, and looking straight into the fire, I knew somehow that my friend A. H. was standing at my left elbow, but so far behind me as to be hidden by the armchair in which I was leaning back. Moving my eyes round slightly without otherwise changing my position, the lower portion of one leg became visible, and I instantly recognized the grey-blue material of trousers he often wore, but the stuff appeared

[11] There is, however, a case in which an apparition, though close in front of the mirror, showed *no* reflection (*J*. x. 308).

semi-transparent, reminding me of tobacco smoke in consistency. I could have touched it with my hand without moving more than my left arm. With that curious instinctive wish not to see more of such a 'figure,' I did no more than glance once or twice at the apparition and then directed my gaze steadily at the fire in front of me. An appreciable space of time passed—probably several seconds in all, but seeming in reality much longer—when the most curious thing happened. Standing upright between me and the window on my left, and at a distance of about four feet from me and almost immediately behind my chair, I saw perfectly distinctly the figure of my friend—the face very pale, the head slightly thrown back, the eyes shut, and on one side of the throat, just under the jaw, a wound with blood on it. The figure remained motionless with the arms close to the sides, and for some time, how long I can't say, I looked steadily at it; then all at once I roused myself, turned deliberately round, the figure vanished, and I realized instantly that I had seen the figure behind me without moving from my first position— an impossible feat physically. I am perfectly certain I never moved my position from the first appearance of the figure as seen physically, until it disappeared on my turning round."

The percipient's friend had fainted and fallen down in the street, receiving a wound in the throat, from which he recovered.

It looks as if the constructor of the apparition, trying to play the game and imitate normal, optical laws as far as the field of vision was concerned, lost patience when the percipient steadily refused to cooperate by turning round, and revealed that an apparition *can* be seen as well "through the back of the head" as in any other direction. The apparition is quite evidently, therefore, a constructed play, or drama, whose theme it is to imitate the normal; and its power of doing so is altogether phenomenal.

4.  ADDITIONAL FEATURES

A characteristic of apparitions, which has given rise to some confusion, not to say ridicule, is that the central figure does not appear alone. It appears with clothes on; and people have asked whether, in addition to believing in ghosts, they are expected to believe in ghostly skirts and ghostly trousers! The answer supplied by the evidence is quite definite. They are not only expected to believe in ghostly skirts and trousers, but also in ghostly hats, sticks, dogs, horses, carriages, doors, curtains—anything, in fact, with which a human being is commonly surrounded. The difficulty in accepting these things is not really a difficulty at all. It arises from a false conception of what an apparition is.

CASE 30 Two brothers, having married two sisters, lived in houses a mile and a quarter apart in a sparsely inhabited part of the Norfolk Fen district. A friend who was staying with one of the families, looking out of the window at about 4 o'clock in the afternoon said, "Here is your brother coming." His account continues, "My host advanced to the window and said, 'Oh, yes, here he is; and see, Robert has got Dobbin out at last.' Dobbin was a horse, which on account of some accident, had not been used for some weeks. The lady also looked out of the window, and said to me, 'And I am so glad, too, that my sister is with him. They will be delighted to find you here.' I recognized distinctly the vehicle in which they rode as being an open one, also the lady and gentleman, and both their dress and their attitudes.

"Our friends passed at a gentle pace along the front of the window, and then, turning with the road round the corner of the house, they could no longer be seen. After a minute my host went to the door and exclaimed, "Why, what can be the matter? They have gone on without calling, a thing they never did in their lives before. What can be the matter?" Five minutes afterwards, while we were seated by the fireside, the parlour door opened, and there entered a lady of about 25 years of age; she was in robust health and in full possession of all her senses, and she was possessed besides of strong common sense. She was pale and much excited, and . . . exclaimed, 'Oh, aunt, I have had such a fright. Father and mother have passed me on the road without speaking. I looked up at them as they passed by, but they looked straight on and never stopped nor said a word. A quarter of an hour before, when I started to walk here, they were sitting by the fire; and now what can be the matter? They never turned or spoke, and yet I am certain that they must have seen me.'

"Ten minutes after the arrival of this lady, I, looking through the window up the road, said, 'But see, here they are, coming down the road again.' My host said, 'No, that is impossible, because there is no path by which they could get on to this road, so as to be coming down it again. But sure enough, here they are, and with the same horse! How in the world have they got here?' "

This time they really arrived, having left their stable about the time the apparition was seen.

Here, then, the apparition comprised, not only two human figures, but also a horse and trap.

It will be unnecessary to give many detailed quotations from cases illustrating this point. In Case 32 below, Canon Bourne is seen riding his well-known horse, Paddy, and waving his hat. A rector is seen accompanied by his dog.[12] A fisherman, fishing with rod and line.[13] A choirman holding out a roll of music.[14] The percipient's great-uncle, holding a roll of paper and a stick.[15] Two school-girls had exchanged rings and made a compact that whichever died first should send back the ring to the other. One of them appears to the other, holding out the ring.[16] A carriage and pair, with two men on the box and a figure inside.[17] Two native servants appear with the chief figure, roll up his bed and take it away.[18] The figure of St. Stanislaus appears in company of a Catholic youth who has just died.[19] And the environment can be more comprehensive than this. In one case the percipient not only saw her father on horseback but saw him in a plantation which was completely out of sight from the place where she was standing.[20]

CASE 31 In Sir Ernest Bennett's book, *Apparitions and Haunted Houses,* an interesting example occurs. In his Case 102, Miss Ruth Wynne, writing from Rougham Rectory, Bury St. Edmunds, in March 1934, reports as follows. "I came to live at Rougham, four miles from Bury St. Edmunds, in 1926. The district was then entirely new to me, and I and

12 *Proc.* xxxiii. 387.  15 *P.L.* (211).      18 *Proc.* v. 433.
13 *Proc.* xxxiii. 376.  16 *P.L.* (514).      19 *P.L.* (349).
14 *H.P.* (726).         17 *H.P.* 654 B.     20 Case 32, pp. 77-78.

my pupil, a girl of 14, spent our afternoon walks exploring it. One dull, damp afternoon, I think in October 1926, we walked off through the fields to look at the church of the neighbouring village, Bradfield St. George. In order to reach the church, which we could see plainly ahead of us to the right, we had to pass through a farmyard, whence we came out on to a road. We had never previously taken this particular walk, nor did we know anything about the topography of the hamlet of Bradfield St. George. Exactly opposite us on the further side of the road and flanking it, we saw a high wall of greenish-yellow bricks. The road ran past us for a few yards, then curved away from us to the left. We walked along the road, following the brick wall round the bend, where we came upon tall, wrought-iron gates set in the wall. I think the gates were shut, or one side may have been open. The wall continued on from the gates and disappeared round the curve of the road. Behind the wall, and towering above it, was a cluster of tall trees. From the gates a drive led away among these trees to what was evidently a large house. We could just see a corner of the roof above a stucco front, in which I remembered noticing some windows of Georgian design. The rest of the house was hidden by the branches of the trees. We stood by the gates for a moment, speculating as to who lived in this large house, and I was rather surprised that I had not already heard of the owner amongst the many people who had called on my mother since our arrival in the district. . . . My pupil and I did not take the same walk again until the following spring. It was, as far as I can remember, a dull afternoon, with good visibility, in February or March. We walked up through the farmyard as before, and out on to the road, where, suddenly, we both stopped dead of one accord and gasped. 'Where's the wall?' we queried simultaneously. It was not there. The road was flanked by nothing but a ditch, and beyond the ditch lay a wilderness of tumbled earth, weeds, mounds, all overgrown with the trees which we had seen on our first visit. We followed the road on round the bend, but there were no gates, no drive, no corner of a house to be seen. We were both very puzzled. At first we thought that our house and wall had been pulled down since our last visit, but closer inspection showed a pond and other small pools amongst the mounds where the house had been visible. It was obvious that they had been there a long time." No one in the neighbourhood had ever heard of the house. Miss Allington, the pupil, adds her corroborative statement.

The case brings to mind the experiences, described in *An Adventure*, of Miss Moberly and Miss Jourdain in the gardens at Versailles.

It is clear from all these cases that there is no difference in existential status between one part of an apparition and another. In ..whatever sense the central figure is "there," the auxiliary objects, the additional figures, and the environment are "there" too. They all come about in the same way, and the central figure has no greater reality and no different kind of reality from the other figures or accompanying objects. Apparitional dramas need no more be confined to the portrayal of a single human figure than need a cinematograph film.

The situation is rather a strange one because, although nothing is *physically* present in space, something (a *visual* solid) *is visibly* present in physical space. An apparition is therefore a thing of great interest.

## 5.  COLLECTIVE PERCIPIENCE

A great stumbling-block in the way of an explanation of telepathic apparitions has been the fact that some of them are collectively perceived. I have counted 130 collective cases, and have no doubt that this list is not exhaustive. In one sense it is true that collective percipience is not very common, for the collective cases do not form a large percentage of the total number. In the Census of Hallucinations it was found that the collective cases formed about 8 per cent of the total; but when we come to realize the nature of collective percipience that is easily accounted for. It is because, when the sight of an apparition is shared, it is shared by the bystanders; and in a large number of cases the percipient is alone at the time of his experience, and the case is not collective because there is no one to share it. Given the presence of more than one person when an apparition is seen, collective percipience is not particularly rare. Gurney says that "the cases where the experience has been shared by a second person appear to be more numerous than those where a second person has been present, awake and rightly situated, and has not shared the experience." But from the Census figures it would appear that only about one third of such cases are collective.

The theories put forward by Gurney and Myers to explain collective percipience have already been discussed. The main difficulty is to understand why a telepathic apparition should be shared by two or more people simply because they happen to be on the spot, regardless of whether or not they are in sympathy with the agent or even acquainted with him. Gurney thought that the telepathic message was received and externalized by the one percipient for whom it was intended by the agent, and then telepathically passed on from one percipient to another. Myers thought that the agent was "metetherially," though not physically, present in space where the apparition was seen. The real crux of the difficulty is not merely that each of the percipients sees at the same time an apparition *more or less* similar to that which the others see; it is that all the percipients see the *same* thing, each from his own point of view in space, just as though it were a material figure. Gurney, apparently, half doubted whether this were so; but I do not think that the evidence, carefully looked into, leaves any reasonable doubt that it is.

Case 32   Take this case. Canon Bourne and his two daughters are out hunting, and the daughters decide to return home with the coachman while their father goes on. "As we were turning to go home," say the two Miss Bournes in a joint account, "we distinctly saw my father, waving his hat to us and signing us to follow him. He was on the side of a small hill, and there was a dip between him and us. My sister, the coachman and myself all recognized my father, and also the horse. The horse looked so dirty and shaken that the coachman remarked he thought there had been a nasty accident. As my father waved his hat I clearly saw the Lincoln and Bennett mark inside, though from the distance we were apart it ought to have been utterly impossible for me to have seen it. . . . Fearing an accident, we hurried down the hill. From the nature of the ground we had to lose sight of my father, but it took us very few seconds to reach the place where we had seen him. When we got there, there was no sign of him anywhere, nor could we see anyone in sight at all. We rode about for some time looking for him, but could not see or hear anything of him. We all reached home within a quarter of an hour of each other. My father then told us he had never been in the field, nor near the field, in which we thought we saw him, the whole of that day. He had never waved to us, and had met with no accident. My father was riding the only white horse that was out that day." A similar appearance of Canon Bourne was seen on another occasion.

It seems very improbable that three people should ride by common consent towards a figure on horseback, comparing notes as to the condition of the horse, if they were seeing three separate and independent figures, and not discover the fact.

CASE 33 Two brothers, occupying a cabin in an old-time naval ship, were sleeping in cots hung parallel to one another. "Both brothers must have been awaked suddenly and simultaneously—by what they never knew—by some irresistible and unknown power—waked to see standing between their cots the figure of their father. Both gazed in mute amazement: there it stood, motionless for a moment, which seemed a century; then it raised one hand and pointed to its own eyes. They were closed. My brother," says the narrator, "started up in bed, and as he did so the form vanished." Their father died about that time.

If two people see an apparitional figure standing between them, it is surely highly probable that they see the *same* figure, one from each side. The fact that two people are looking at the same figure could only be established by very exact and detailed description, such as in ordinary life we do not supply. We do not, for example, say, "I see a man who is facing away from me and about 45 degrees to the left of my line of sight"; and I do not think we can expect percipients of apparitions to give similarly detailed descriptions of the figures they see, so as to prove that they see the same figure. But we know that in the case of a single percipient, the figure varies as the percipient moves round it, or, what comes to the same thing, as the figure moves across the percipient's field of vision, in accordance with the physical laws of perspective and distance. We know also that in cases of collective percipience the different percipients see the figure in the same *place,* and are always, or almost always, in agreement as to what they see. It seems therefore that there is scarcely room for doubt that the sensory image of one percipient is correlated with the sensory image of another just as it would be if the two percipients were seeing the same material figure in normal perception. There are quite a number of instances in which ghosts have been seen collectively, as well as crisis-apparitions, and there is nothing to suggest that different figures are being seen by the different percipients. The following is to the point from the record of the Morton ghost (Case 16). "My sister E. was singing in the back drawing-room. I heard her stop abruptly, come out into the hall and call me. She said she had seen the figure in the drawing-room, close behind her as she sat at the piano. I went back into the room with her, and saw the figure in the bow window in the usual place. I spoke to her several times but had no answer. She stood there for about ten minutes or a quarter of an hour; then went across the room to the door, and along the passage, disappearing in the same place by the garden door. My sister then came in from the garden, saying she had seen her coming up the kitchen steps outside. We all three then went out into the garden, when Mrs. K. called from a window on the first storey that she had just seen her pass across the lawn in front, and along the carriage drive towards the orchard. This evening, then, altogether four people saw her." It is true that the figure was seen successively and not collectively on this occasion. But it looks very much as if the visual images of the four percipients were correlated with one another and not independent of one another.

A case illustrating the fact that the percipient may walk round an apparition and see it as if it were a material figure from different angles and distances will be found in *Phantasms of the Living* (Case 210). The percipient saw the apparition first from his bed; then from the window; then (having walked right through it) from the door.

If it be granted, as I think it reasonably must be, that perception of apparitions is full-blown perception, identical in its features with normal perception, and that in collective cases the various percipients see the *same* figure, each appropriately according to his position and distance from the figure; and that, as the figure moves, the sensory images of all the percipients change exactly as they would if the figure were a material one, then Gurney's theory of collective perception breaks down. For it might be conceived that one percipient should telepathically affect another so as to cause him to see a figure *more or less* like the one he was seeing himself, but it is inconceivable that the figures should be exactly correlated to one another as in normal perception. Indeed, experimental telepathy suggests that the figures seen by the different percipients would be likely to differ a good deal from one another.

We have then this fact of the collective percipience of apparitions, full of significance for the theory. *The visual solid constituting the apparition is provided by the percipient.* And in collective cases each percipient is providing the aspect of this visual solid appropriate to his own situation in space. Astonishing as it seems, these independently provided aspects are as exactly correlated to one another as they are in normal vision. Looked at from the human point of view of conscious planning, this appears to be something like a miracle. Moreover, the "miracle" is not confined to collective percipience. It occurs again in mirror-images of apparitions; in adjustment to lighting and distance, and in the exact correlation and sequence of visible aspects as the figure moves across the field of vision of a single percipient. But of course, although all this is brought about, it is not consciously planned in the human sense.

## 6. FEELING OF COLD

Another characteristic of apparitions, not invariably but fairly frequent, is that the percipients experience a feeling of cold. One can see no reason for these cold feelings; they are just an empirical fact.[21] But the consensus of statements

[21] *If* it be a fact that supernormal phenomena of a physical nature occur, and *if* they are accompanied by a physical fall of temperature, it is just possible that those which accompany some apparitions may be imitative.

about them further endorses the truth of the accounts. It will be sufficient to give a string of extracts from cases on this point without giving the reference to each case. "I . . . felt myself grow perfectly cold." The experience was like "a jug of cold water poured on the nape of the neck." "As if the blood was like ice in my veins." "A cold, shivering feeling came over me." The apparition "laid a cold hand on his cheek." "Her kiss was like a waft of cold air upon my cheek." "She felt a cold hand clasp hers." "I awoke in a cold sweat." The percipient "felt an icy wind blowing." "As if a cool wind was blowing about me." "As the figure passed we distinctly felt a cold air." Again, "An icy chill passed through him, and his hair bristled." "My hair seemed to bristle." (Cf Job iv. 15, "Then a spirit passed before my face; and the hair of my flesh stood up.")

It seems probable that these cold feelings are subjective. Again, the Morton ghost supplies evidence of this. "I felt a cold icy shiver," says Miss E. Morton as the ghost bent over her whilst she was playing the piano. On another occasion footsteps were heard to pass Miss Morton, her mother, and a maid. They saw nothing but most of them "felt an icy shiver." When a party of five, consisting of two Miss Mortons and three of the maids, were standing outside their bedrooms with their candles alight, listening to the footsteps, "walking up and down the landing between them," they felt "a cold wind, though their candles were not blown about." This surely must have been a subjective feeling of a wind, and not a physical cold wind. It is possible that the act of supernormal perception brings about physiological changes which might lower the temperature of the body. Notice that in one of the *experimental cases*,[22] the percipient says, "I felt a cold breath streaming over me, and violent palpitation of the heart came on."

### 7. OTHER SUBJECTIVE FEELINGS

Sometimes in addition to the feeling of cold, but often without it, other subjective feelings are experienced by percipients of apparitions. People who were asleep often say that they

[22] *P.L.* I. pp. lxxxi-iv.

were suddenly awakened by something before they saw the apparition. Or they have had a feeling of a presence. I will again quote from a few cases merely the relevant sentences. "My eyes were fixed on my book, when suddenly I *felt*, but did not *see*, some one come into my room."[23] "I now became aware of my husband's presence at the door of my room, then of his presence filling the chamber and slowly and solemnly crossing to the bed where I lay."[24] "I woke up with a start, and an idea that some one had come into the room."[25] "I felt as if I had been aroused intentionally."[26] "I . . . was thoroughly absorbed in my book . . . when suddenly without a moment's warning my whole being seemed roused to the highest state of tension and aliveness, and I was aware, with an intenseness not easily imagined by those who have never experienced it, that another being or presence was not only in the room but close to me."[27] "She woke up with a feeling of a presence in the room."[28] "I have had an odd sensation in summer, early in the morning, that there was a woman in the room, but I could not look up till she was gone. I considered this to be a species of nightmare, till last August, I was, as before, lying awake when the same feeling came over me; this time far more strongly. I heard a dress rustle, and *felt* a short, dark woman was coming towards my bed. She put her hand on my shoulder, etc."[29]

The feeling of presence is found even in experimental cases. The following occurred during some interesting experimental attempts by Mr. J. Kirk to make his apparition visible to a certain Miss G. "I have twice since succeeded in impressing her," he says. "The first time was about three weeks ago . . . and the second on Sunday night, the 11th inst. On the first occasion she had a distinct feeling that I was standing by her bedside, and the presence was so palpable (though unseen) that she felt the pressure on the bedstead. Miss G. describes this pressure and presence as like those one feels when some one is leaning on the back of an easy chair in which you are sitting."[30]

[23] *P.L.* (295).       [26] *P.L.* (426 A).       [29] *Proc.* iii. 114.
[24] *P.L.* (644).       [27] *H.P.* (665 A).        [30] *J.* v. 20-31.
[25] *P.L.* I. p. lxxxii.  [28] *Proc.* xxxiii. 384.

It sounds as though the palpable presence was some kind of direct sensing, while the feeling of pressure was a hallucination of the sense of touch. In other cases the percipients emphasize the *indescribableness* of their sensations. It may be that, whereas a hallucination of the senses imitates normal perception, these indescribable experiences are inklings of a new kind of perception altogether, which finds no replica in normal life. The evidence for this faculty of being able to sense a presence, though not, perhaps, large in amount, is not negligible. In a surprising number of cases the percipient mentions feelings which it is very difficult to describe. These all suggest that hallucinations are not bound to confine themselves to reproducing normal perceptions, but that they usually do so because it is demanded by the agent's idea.

To recapitulate, apparitions have been divided into four classes: (1) Experimental, (2) Crisis-apparitions, (3) Postmortem Cases, (4) Ghosts. Running more or less through all these classes, seven important characteristics have been noticed and illustrated by examples. (i) The different ways in which apparitions externalize themselves in space. (ii) The fact that apparitions have no physical basis. (iii) The way in which apparitions deliberately imitate normal percepts, when in fact they are not obliged to do so. (iv) The fact that apparitions include all kinds of additional features besides the central figure, and that the additions and the central figure all come into existence in the same way. (v) The fact that apparitions, both visual and auditory, are sometimes collective. (vi) The cold feelings which sometimes accompany apparitions. (vii) Certain subjective feelings sometimes accompanying apparitions, which may possibly be quasi-percepts of an unfamiliar kind.

All the characteristics do not, of course, appear in every case: in fact, apparitions give one the impression of being phenomena which attain expression in a fragmentary and imperfect way only. And they show an individual originality and contempt for rule which makes them not easy to classify. Moreover, some percipients are better than others, and some seem to be almost incapable of perceiving an apparition at all. There is also a variation in the power of percipience with the same individual from time to time. Nearly all the cases on record are incomplete in one way or another, and the number of cases in which the three senses of sight, hearing, and touch have all been hallucinated together is very small. Compared with the marvellous perfection of normal sense-perception, the perception of apparitions is a very amateur performance indeed. But it is profoundly instructive.

## 8. THE PARTICIPATION OF ANIMALS IN TELEPATHY

Before leaving these illustrative cases, it may not be out of place to say something about the relation of animals to telepathic phenomena. In a number of cases dogs have provided evidence of seeing the figures seen by human beings in haunted houses, and they often appear to be terrified by them. There are also cases in which apparitions of dogs and cats have been seen. One of the best examples I have come across of the entry of the animal mind into telepathic phenomena is that of Rider Haggard's dog.

CASE 34   One night Rider Haggard had what at first he took to be a nightmare. "I was awakened," he says, "by my wife's voice calling to me from her own bed upon the other side of the room. As I awoke, the nightmare itself, which had been long and vivid, faded from my brain. All I could remember of it was a sense of awful oppression and of desperate and terrified struggling for life such as the act of drowning would probably involve. But between the time when I heard my wife's voice and the time that my consciousness answered to it, or so it seemed to me, I had another dream. I dreamed that a black retriever dog, a most amiable and intelligent beast named Bob . . . was lying on its side among brushwood, or rough growth of some sort, by water. My own personality in some mysterious way seemed to me to be arising from the body of the dog, which I knew quite surely to be Bob and no other, so much so that my head was against his head, which was lifted up at an unnatural angle. In my vision the dog was trying to speak to me in words, and, failing, transmitted to my mind in an undefined fashion the knowledge that it was dying. Then everything vanished, and

I woke to hear my wife asking me why on earth I was making those horrible and weird noises. I replied that I had had a nightmare about a fearful struggle, and that I had dreamed that old Bob was in a dreadful way, and was trying to talk to me and to tell me about it."

Railway men found the dog's collar on an openwork bridge over some water, and it appeared that the dog had been struck by a passing train in the night and thrown down into the water below. Its body was found three days later. The percipient said that he never remembers having had any other telepathic dream.

If the case be accepted as telepathic, it means that those mid-level elements of personality, which, on the present view, are responsible for telepathic contacts, exist in the case of dogs as well as in the case of human beings.

## 9. THE "PERFECT APPARITION"

Since the characteristics of apparitions straggle through a large number of cases, it is not easy to appreciate their full significance while they are strung out in this attenuated form. I propose therefore to collect them together by the device of creating an imaginary apparition which shall exhibit all the chief characteristics at once, and this I shall call the "Perfect Apparition." The figure is imaginary only in one sense. Each of its features rests on solid evidence; but they are not all to be found in any actual single case, although there are cases which contain a good many of them. The "Perfect Apparition" is a useful aid to realizing the sort of thing an apparition is.

The references given by no means constitute the whole of the evidence in support of each characteristic of the apparition, but are examples only. There is not much evidence, however, for items (5) and (10).

Let us suppose, for purposes of comparison, that the "Perfect Apparition" is standing beside a normal human being. We should find the following points of resemblance:

(1) Both figures would stand out in space and would appear equally real and solid. The apparition would be just as

clear and vivid in matters of detail, such as the colour and texture and clothing, as the material person.[31]

(2) We should be able to walk round the apparition, viewing it from any distance and from any standpoint, and as regards distance and perspective we should detect no difference between it and the living person.[32]

(3) If the light happened to be poor, both figures would be badly seen, and if more light were turned on, both figures would appear brighter. If the light went out, both figures would disappear in the darkness.[33]

(4) Both figures would obscure the background.[34]

(5) If the apparition happened to be wearing a rose in its buttonhole, we should probably smell the scent of it.[35]

(6) On approaching the apparition, we should hear it breathing, and we should hear the rustle of its clothes as it moved and its shoes would shuffle on the floor.[36]

(7) The apparition would probably behave as if aware of our presence, looking at us in a natural way and possibly smiling and turning its head to follow our movements. It might even place its hand on our shoulder, in which case we should feel an ordinary human touch.[37]

(8) The apparition might speak to us, and possibly it might go as far as to answer a question; but we should not be able to engage it in any long conversation.[38]

(9) If a mirror were fixed to the wall we should see the apparition reflected in it at the appropriate angle, just as we should see the reflection of the real man.[39]

(10) Both figures would probably cast shadows, but the evidence on this point is uncertain.[40]

(11) If we were to shut our eyes or turn away our head,

[31] *H.P.* (714); *Proc.* vi. 17; *Proc.* xxxiii. 168 and 374; *J.* vi. 230.
[32] *P.L.* (349), (357), (665); *Proc.* iii. 126; *Proc.* viii. 311-29; *J.* v. 223-6.
[33] *H.P.* (645), (2); *Proc.* vi. 27; *Proc.* viii. 313 and 326.
[34] *Proc.* vi. 128-32, and most cases.
[35] *P.L.* (18); *J.* xii. 188-90.
[36] *P.L.* (312); *Proc.* iii. 123 and 134; *J.* iv. 286.
[37] *P.L.* (29), (210); *Proc.* viii. 214; *Proc.* xxxiii. 168.
[38] All cases in which the apparition speaks, of which there are many examples.
[39] *H.P.* (428 E); *J.* v. 223; *J.* vi. 145 and 286; *J.* x. 308.
[40] *Proc.* iii. 121; *J.* xvi. 282.

the apparition would disappear just as the figure by its side would do. And on reopening them, we should see it again.[41]

(12) In addition to its clothes, the figure might have other accessories, such as a stick or any other object. And it might be accompanied by a dog or even by another human being. These would appear normal and behave in a normal manner. With regard to a human companion, I do not think it would make any difference whether he had ever existed or not. Mr. Pickwick or Sherlock Holmes would probably do as well as Charles Dickens or Sir Arthur Conan Doyle, and would appear just as alive and natural.[42]

(13) The apparition might pick up any object in the room or open and close the door. We should both see and hear these objects moved: yet physically they would never have moved at all.[43]

In all these points the apparition's imitation of a material figure would be perfect. But we should find points of difference no less striking.

(14) For one thing, as soon as we came near the apparition, or if the apparition touched us, we might feel a sensation of cold.[44]

(15) If we tried to take hold of the apparition, our hand would go through it without encountering any resistance. In the most perfect case I am not quite sure about this, for the sensation of touch is undoubtedly hallucinated in such cases, and it might be that we should *feel* our hand stopped at the surface of the apparition's body, as by something impenetrable; but at the same time should *see* our hand go right through it without let or hindrance. Apparitions when cornered avoid this interesting situation by disappearing.[45]

(16) If we were to sprinkle French chalk on the floor and could induce the apparition and the human being to walk on it together, we should find that only the real man left any footprints, although we should hear the footsteps of both.[46]

[41] *H.P.* (645 B); (716 C) (2); (725 A); (742 A).
[42] *P.L.* (211), (349); *H.P.* (645 D); (654 A, B); (726).
[43] *Proc.* v. 433; *Proc.* xxxiii. 376 and 387.
[44] *P.L.* (28), (194), (223), (286), (628), (629).
[45] *P.L.* (210), (662); *Proc.* iii. 123; *Proc.* xxxiii. 175; *J.* iv. 286; *J.* vi. 135.
[46] *P.L.* (34).

(17) If we were to take a photograph of the two figures, only the real man would come out. And if we had sound-recording apparatus, only the sounds made by the real man would be recorded. It is true that these are inferences and do not rest on direct evidence. But the non-physical character of apparitions is so clear that the inference seems to be inescapable.

(18) After a time, which might be anything up to half an hour or so, the apparition would disappear. It might suddenly vanish; or it might become transparent and fade away; it might vanish into the wall or go down through the floor, or it might, more conventionally, open the door and walk out.[47]

(19) Sometimes we should probably find that the apparition did not imitate the behaviour of the material man quite so closely. It might, for instance, become slightly luminous; it might show small details of itself when we were so far away from it that normally we could not possibly have seen them; it might even so far forget itself as to make us see it through the back of our head.[48]

This is a picture of what an apparition would be like at its best, according to our collected evidence; and this is what, throughout the ages, has been called a "spirit." But clearly it is in reality a psychological phenomenon, the explanation of which must be sought in the processes of sense-perception.

## 10. BEARING OF THE "PERFECT APPARITION" ON THE VALUE OF THE EVIDENCE

Before delving into the difficult subject of sense-perception, however, let us note that the "Perfect Apparition" has an important bearing on the strength of the evidence on which it is based. It was pointed out above that apparitional cases form a natural group—a fact long ago stressed by Gurney. But now, with the "Perfect Apparition" before us, we can see much more clearly what he meant by this. All the stories combine to describe an apparition having two apparently contradictory characteristics. The group-characteristics embodied in the "Perfect Apparition" are those of a collection of some

[47] *Proc.* ii. 141; *Proc.* viii. 315; *J.* vi. 231.
[48] *H.P.* (645 D), (665 A); *J.* v. 224.

hundreds of narratives sent in by independent witnesses. How is it that these independent narratives conspire to describe phenomena having two characteristics which, to common sense, seem to contradict one another? These characteristics are, (i) the apparition imitates the behaviour of a normal, material figure with almost miraculous fidelity, appealing convincingly to the senses of sight, hearing, and touch and behaving at the same time as if it were conscious of what it is doing; yet all the while (ii) the apparition proves itself to be a non-physical phenomenon, or, in ordinary language, it proves that there is "nothing there." Would any ordinary person, drawing on his imagination to make a good story, string together two such apparent contradictions? It is true that these two characteristics are not really contradictory, but it takes a fairly profound expedition into philosophy to show how they are compatible. Can we credit the contributors of these cases with having thought out an apparition having these contradictory qualities and arranged that all their stories should conspire to describe it? The suggestion is obviously fantastic, especially since the contributors of the stories were strangers to one another and many of them were not even contemporaries. Moreover, the ghost stories of fiction show no sign that their authors have even dimly conceived the idea of a visible, audible, and tangible, yet non-physical ghost. In hear-say stories apparitions leave physical traces behind them, and the narrators appear to be unconscious that there is any reason why they should not. In one fairly well-known story of an apparition, which has been broadcast on the wireless, the figure of an unknown man was seen on board ship sitting in the captain's cabin. It disappeared, but writing was found to have been entered in the log-book telling the captain to put the ship on a certain course. This was done, and presently a party of people was rescued from an iceberg. One of the party was like the figure seen in the cabin and his handwriting resembled that in the log-book. This is what apparitions do in fictitious stories but do not do in well-evidenced cases such as those of our own collection. Of course there is a temptation to bring in the physical trace, which remains to prove the story.

If our spontaneous stories of apparitions are unreliable, how is this difference to be accounted for? It seems that we must assume either that (a) the authors of the narratives deliberately conspired together to give the apparitions the characteristics (i) and (ii) above; or that (b) they simply drew on their imaginations and their stories happened to conform to these characteristics by chance. Both these theories are surely too obviously absurd to be worth discussing. There may possibly be some critics who hold that anything can be legitimately put down to chance unless a probability-figure can be quoted to prove the opposite. To take up such a position is surely to lack a sense of reality. It resembles the attitude of a man who refuses to step on to a street grating without first measuring the width of his body and the width of the slots in the grating, solemnly declaring that until he knows these measurements he cannot be sure that he will not fall through!

If the theories (a) and (b) are both rejected, how can the group-characteristics be accounted for except on the view that the narrators were simply speaking the truth and their accounts all agreed because they were all describing a real phenomenon? The criticism so often brought against spontaneous evidence, that the narrators' memories failed them, that the essential parts of the story were read back into it afterwards, that the narrator embroidered, and so on, must be accompanied by an explanation of why it is that the apparitions all possess the characteristics (i) and (ii)—that is to say that together they describe the "Perfect Apparition"—before it becomes plausible. These group-characteristics are, in fact, the strongest evidence for the validity of the spontaneous cases, and it is worth while to emphasize this fact. Anyone who suggests that the spontaneous evidence is invalid must begin by accounting for the presence of these two group-characteristics.

# Chapter III

## Theory of Apparitions

### 1. NORMAL SENSE-PERCEPTION

THE APPARITION, once admitted to be a fact, presents a very interesting problem in sense-perception. But, before describing the kind of phenomenon it appears to be, it will be necessary to place before the reader a brief outline of the nature of normal sense-perception, though this will not be needed by those already familiar with the subject. For the present purpose the main thing to grasp is that, in certain important respects, material things are not what they seem. If we are looking at a common object, such as a brick, we *feel* that, in the act of looking at it, we are being made directly aware of the existence of a brick and of some of its properties. *There is,* we say, a brick about such a distance away—an oblong-shaped, solid object with square corners, reddish in colour and having a rough surface. We say this without any feeling of doubt. In fact, to the person who is entirely unacquainted with the philosophy of sense-perception, it probably seems absurd to suggest that there is anything in it to argue about. His view is that "seeing is believing." We feel that in this act of vision we *know* that the brick is there and what it is like. But, in fact, we do not *know* this. The feeling we have is not *knowledge* but only *belief*. We may, after all, be mistaken. The object may turn out not to be a brick at all but a very skilfully made cardboard imitation. And even if we are right about its being a real brick, reflection shows that we cannot be right in our conviction that we are *directly* aware of it *as it now is*. For time must have elapsed since the light left it which now reaches our eyes; and more time still must have been taken by the nervous stimuli engendered in the optical processes of vision to travel from our eyes to our brain. The total time no doubt is very short in the case of a brick or of any object near at hand: but if it is a star we are looking at, thousands of years may have elapsed since the light left it which now reaches us; and for all we know the star we think we are seeing *now* may be no longer in existence. At best, therefore, we do not see things as they *are* but as they *were*.

Again, in looking at a brick, although we have the impression of being aware of the brick as a complete object, we are not, and never can be, simultaneously acquainted with the whole of its surface, or with the inside, although all these exist at the same time. Nor were we visibly acquainted with the brick before it entered our field of view: nor shall we be after we have ceased to look at it: yet we never doubt that the brick remains in continuous existence. Sensation is therefore fragmentary both in respect of space and time, whereas the brick is supposed to be a temporally continuous, three-dimensional whole. Vision does not, therefore, give us *direct acquaintance* with material things, as, in looking at them, we believe that it does. It only gives us indirect information about them, and this in a piecemeal manner. In perception we go ahead of our data.

Look at the matter from another angle. If we walk about and look at the brick from different points of view, the image of the brick formed on the retina of our eye will vary according to our position and distance, and the accompanying state of the cells in the visual centre of the brain will vary according to this retinal image. Our seeing of the brick is not, therefore, dependent merely on the intrinsic character of the brick itself, but on a long chain of causes and effects taking place partly in ourselves and partly in the external world, the last term of which is a particular state of a portion of the brain. Hence, we are not, in vision, being made *directly aware* of the brick, because anything which interfered with this chain of causes and effects at any point would interfere with our vision and possibly distort it without there being necessarily any change in the brick: also, anything other than a brick which produced exactly the same state in the cells of our brain as that which this chain of causes and effects produces, would result in our "seeing" the brick, even if there were no brick for us to see. Professor Broad expresses this by saying that vision is not "prehensive." But vision does *claim* to be prehensive. It is that claim which makes it seem absurd to question its processes. But when we do question them, we find the claim to be delusive.

There is, however, one element of vision (and indeed of all sense-perception) about which no mistake is possible. When we look at a brick we are immediately aware of a coloured patch of a particular shape, size, and tint standing at a certain distance away from us in space. On this point there can be no delusion. Whether or not we mistakenly believe this patch to be part of the surface of a brick when, in fact, it is part of the surface of something else, or of no object at all, we cannot be mistaken about being aware of the patch. Either it is present to our consciousness or it is not. We are here in the region of *knowledge* and not of *belief*. This element in the process of vision, which can be separated out of the whole act of perception, is a datum on which the act of perception rests. It is not, of course, separate from perception or antecedent to it. It is an integral constituent of it. The coloured patch is called a "sensum" or "sense-datum;" and the act of being aware of it is called "sensing." With the other senses it is the same. There is a thermal sense-datum, which is the objective constituent of a feeling of warmth or cold. There is an auditory sense-datum, which is a noise. There is an olfactory sense-datum, which is a smell, and a gustatory sense-datum, which is a taste. All these sense-data are correlated with brain-states, on which, in normal perception, they appear to depend. None of the senses is therefore prehensive, whether it purports to be so or not.

The distinction between "sensing" and "perceiving" is not one which we draw in ordinary life. It is a technical distinction recognized by philosophers, important for the analysis of normal sense-perception. It is important also for the present theory of apparitions. *Sensing* gives indisputable knowledge, gained from sensation in the act of sensing a sense-datum. *Perception* is a mental act built on the foundation of direct acquaintance by sensing. It is an act which *takes for granted* the existence of a particular material thing forming part of our environment. In perception we *jump* from the *knowledge* that there is a coloured patch or a noise to the *belief* that there is a brick over there or a bell ringing in the distance. This jump is not made by inference: we do not *infer* the existence of a material thing from the sensing of a sense-datum. On sensing the sense-datum we make the jump of uncritically taking for granted that a particular material thing is there. This uncritical taking-for-granted may turn out to be wrong: but awareness of a sense-datum can never be wrong or mistaken.

Now sense-data, as they present themselves to us in perception, claim to be quite literally constituents of material things. To confine ourselves to the visual sense, the reddish, oblong patch, which is the sense-datum we sense when we look at a brick, claims actually to *be* the front surface of the brick. In practical life we never pause to consider this claim; we accept it as obviously true. But a little reflection will show what difficulties confront this common-sense view. If I shut my eyes, the sense-datum ceases to exist, along with the brain-state which generated it. Have I then, by shutting my eyes, annihilated the front surface of the brick? If this be rejected as absurd, how can it be maintained that the sense-datum formed part of the brick's surface?

Again, reflection shows that we are constantly sensing visual sense-data which cannot possibly form parts of the surfaces of material things. For example, if the brick is reflected in a mirror, the mirror-image is a sense-datum; but obviously it forms no part of the brick's surface. Nor, for that matter, does it form part of the surface of the mirror. It forms no part of any material thing at all. Or, if we take an irregular-shaped piece of glass and look at the brick through that, we sense a distorted sense-datum, which cannot form part of the surface of the brick.

Another difficulty arises when the observer moves about. When I look at a brick from a place close to it, I sense a large and detailed sense-datum. But if I look at the brick from a long way off, I sense a small and undetailed sense-datum. How can both these sense-data be literally parts of the brick's surface? And if either of them is, how am I to know which? The problem of vision is evidently a good deal more complicated than everyday experience leads us to believe. And the same is true of touching, hearing, tasting, and smelling. There is no space here in which to go into arguments and counter-arguments which fill volumes. It can only be stated dogmatically that the sense-data sensed by each percipient are *private to himself and originate in processes which take place in his own personality*. They are not constituent elements of material things in any sense which makes them so in independence of the observer, as, in the naïve act of perception, we take it for granted that they are. On the contrary, the material thing is in part the percipient's own construct on account of these sense-data which he supplies.

A further point to be noticed is that there are sense-data which obviously have nothing to do with material things at all, even remotely. These are hallucinatory sense-data, or, again, those we sense in dreams as well as some which mingle with the sense-data of normal perception, forming the partial and minor hallucinations which frequently occur in daily life: and some which form the hallucinations caused by taking certain drugs, such as hasheesh, or are produced in hypnosis. These hallucinatory sense-data differ from the sense-data of normal perception in that the physical sense-organs have nothing to do with their production: but they do not differ from them in any other way. The coloured patch, for example, which forms part of the opium-smoker's vision, is as much a real sense-datum as the one we sense when we look at a brick. How is it that if every sense-datum occurring in normal perception is caused by a particular neural state which is the result of the operation of a sense-organ, and the setting in motion of a sequence of physiological changes, these hallucinatory sense-data can occur when the sense-organs are not operating and therefore cannot be causing these neural states? The answer usually given to this question by philosophers and psychologists is that the neural state in the brain, which would normally be produced by the operation of the sense-organ is, in the case of a hallucination, still there, but that it has been "centrally" instead of "peripherally" initiated. The meaning of this somewhat cryptic phrase is rendered clearer by the following paragraph taken from an article on Hallucinations in the *Encyclopaedia Britannica* (13th edition). "It is generally and rightly assumed," says the writer of the article, "that the hallucinatory perception of any object has for its immediate correlate a state of excitement which, as regards its characters and its distribution in the elements of the brain, is entirely similar to the neural correlate of the normal perception of the same object. The hallucination is a perception, though a false perception." So that whatever state of the brain is correlated with a particular sense-datum in normal perception, an exactly similar state of the brain is brought into existence when a similar sense-datum forms part of a hallucination.

The surprising thing about this is that, although it takes an elaborate sense-organ with much auxiliary nervous mechanism to produce exactly the right brain-state to give rise to the sense-datum in normal perception, this identical brain-state can, if the theory be correct, come into existence without any sense-organ or special nervous mechanism at all! Now the orthodox theory, which the writer in the *Encyclopaedia Britannica* is maintaining, if I understand it rightly, holds that, through repeated acts of normal perception, traces have been left in the brain which act as causal factors in cases of hallucination. And no doubt on such brain-traces would be held to depend the part played by memory in the recognition of objects during perception. The relation of memory to sense-perception is, for the present purpose, a side-issue which cannot be embarked upon: but I find it extremely difficult to understand how brain-traces resulting from, say, repeated observation of the human figure (which must be of the nature of generalized resultants) can possibly give rise to exactly the right neural correlate to produce the sense-datum of a *particular* figure seen from a *particular* angle, such as occurs in the case of an apparition, or, indeed, of any other sensory hallucination. It seems to me that all the facts concerning telepathic apparitions conspire in pointing to their origin as *psychological* and not as *physical*. They do, indeed, *imitate* normal perception with remarkable fidelity; but their not infrequent lapses from fidelity prove that it *is* imitation and not the result of physically based necessity. It looks as though sensory hallucinations are brought about by a quasi-psychological machine—something that lies midway between a mind and a machine, that is to say something with mid-level characteristics. A further difficulty against the physical causation of hallucinations is raised by the collective cases.

Some apparitions, as we have seen, owe their origin to two or more persons who work together with marvellous co-ordination. If the apparitions (or rather the aspects of the same apparition) seen simultaneously by these persons are caused by physical traces in the brain of each, how do the brain-traces in the various brains contrive to get into a state of exact correlation with each other?

Perhaps one need not necessarily abandon the view that brain-traces of some sort accompany sensory hallucinations; and perhaps it may still be maintained that these brain-traces cause the hallucinations. But in that case I see no way of escaping the conclusion that such brain-traces must themselves be *psychologically* caused, so long as it is held that perception is the result of strict causality. There would be two possible views. (1) That sensory hallucinations arise without any physical causal factors, only psychological causation being involved. (2) That sensory hallucinations arise from psychological (mid-level) factors in the personality, which cause *both* the brain-traces and the sense-data as well; or cause the brain-traces which in turn cause the sense-data. The second view is perhaps nearer to orthodoxy; but it increases the marvel of hallucinations. I have suggested, however, that the curious nature of mid-level activities throws open the possibility that the origination of sense-data may not be a strictly causal process, but may depend on something more like conscious response to a signal.

## 2. ILLUSIONS AND HALLUCINATIONS

Perhaps it is worth while here to say something about the relation of illusions to hallucinations and to give some common examples of the latter. Sometimes expectancy or habit give rise to partial hallucinations in daily life. It may happen that one is waiting for a bus and on the look-out for a particular number. A bus with another number approaches but in the distance one sees quite clearly on the front of it the number one is waiting for. One may easily, for example, *see* 74 when the number is 14. The subject of one such hallucination switched on the wireless by the switch on the set, and *saw* the dial light up for a moment and then go out. Examination showed that the current had never been turned on at the wall-switch, so that the dial could never have lit up at all. These are not cases of illusion. They are cases of hallucination. Another well-known example of the same thing is inability to see mistakes in a proof-sheet.

Linked with such ordinary hallucinations as these are the phenomena recorded by writers on *Gestalt* psychology. Imperfect diagrams are seen as perfect because the missing parts have been supplied by the creation of hallucinatory sensedata generated by the force of association. There are also the phenomena of eidetic imagery, in which the mind carries on the complete percept after the object of perception has been removed. In all these cases the sense-data sensed by the subject actually exist, although they are hallucinatory, and the sense-organs have had no hand in producing them. They have been psychologically supplied.

It is maintained by some people that partial hallucinations are really *illusions;* that is to say that they are false conclusions drawn from correct data. This, however, is not borne out by a careful study of the facts. There are such things as illusions, but they involve a different part of the perceptual process. It is of some importance to grasp the difference between a hallucination and an illusion. An illusion consists in jumping to the wrong conclusion from given sense-data. For example, if on a dark night one looks out of the window, and, sensing a vague sense-datum, takes it for granted that a burglar is there when really there is nothing but a bush, that is a case of illusion. The actual sense-datum supplied by the physical process of vision was sensed. But the *expectation* that there might be a lurking burglar in the garden caused the wrong *perceptual* act to be built up on the correct foundation. But when the dial of the wireless set, in the case just mentioned, was seen to be bright when in reality it was dark, that was a case of hallucination. For the sense-datum of the dark dial, which normal perception would have supplied, was inhibited and a hallucinatory bright sense-datum was supplied in its place. There was no *perceptual* error. The bright sensedatum was actually sensed and actually existed. Of course partial hallucinations and illusions may be mixed together, as would have been the case had the illusory burglar been seen with a non-existent dark lantern.

Returning to the subject of normal perception, those particular sense-data which appear to us to form the surfaces of material things—the coloured patches and extended pressures (it must be remembered that only the two senses of sight and touch reveal to us a world of objects extended in space) enclose impenetrable regions of space. *We ourselves* provide these sense-data. What is the nature of the impenetrable regions? These impenetrable regions are what we mean when we speak of "physical objects." It is essential to grasp clearly the difference between a "physical object" and a "material thing" or "total object," for on this the present theory of apparitions depends. If we return to the brick, our visual perception of it, when we look at it, arises from our sensing the reddish patch, which is a visual sense-datum *provided by ourselves*. We touch the brick, and our tactual perception of it arises from our sensing a rough, extended tactual sense-datum, again of our own providing. If the brick were to fall on the floor, we should hear the noise it made; but here again we should be sensing a sound-datum which we ourselves had created. So it is with all the senses. *In perception we are never acquainted with anything but our own sense-data.* Never do we achieve direct acquaintance with the physical object itself, which we suppose to constitute the real brick. The "material brick" is the totality formed by the two factors, *the "physical object" together with the sense-data which we provide.* What, then, is this "physical object"? And since we are never directly acquainted with it, how do we know that it exists? It is the physically occupied region of a material thing, the region which appears to our senses to be impenetrable; and it is this region which we suppose must originate those causal sequences which, acting through our sense-organs, produce in our brains the neural correlates of our sense-data—that is in cases of normal perception. Only in this way do we know that there is a brick at all. We can thus only define the physical object in terms of its power of originating causal sequences; that is, we can only define it in terms of its causal properties. We can infer that one physical object causally affects another. We can, for instance, put a piece of ice on the stove and the stove will cause the ice to change its properties: it will melt it. But notice that even now we only know about the causal properties of physical objects by changes affected in our own sense-data. Hence philosophers distinguish between a "material thing" or "total object" and a "physical object," which is only one factor of the former. In ordinary life we never draw this distinction; in fact, it never occurs to us that the distinction exists. It is not necessary that we should be aware of it in practical life and therefore nature hides it from us. But for an understanding of apparitions it becomes very important.

Notice that the fact that we are only aware of the existence of physical objects by means of sense-data of our own manufacture introduces the theoretical possibility that we might be hoodwinked about the nature of physical objects. If all the sense-data of everybody happened to be the result of some extraordinarily large-scale and perfect hallucination which exactly imitated the operation of physical objects and their causal properties, we should never discover the fact. I do not suggest that this actually is so; but we have seen that a semi-miraculous power of imitation, down to the smallest details, is an outstanding characteristic of sensory hallucinations. As a matter of fact, as long as we possess physical bodies, we appear to have the means of unmasking such hypothetical hallucinations. (See Ch. VI, §1).

One other point is worth mentioning. Where there arise doubts about the nature of the physical world which are due to the nature of sense-perception, it is no use turning to science for an answer or a decision. Whatever doubts infect sense-perception must also infect the whole body of experimental science, which ultimately rests on sense-perception. Scientists no doubt discover a great deal by the use of instruments; but it must be remembered that these are aids to the senses, not substitutes for them. In fact, epistemological questions are of fundamental importance in any search for truth and take precedence of the appeal to experiment.

Having got so far and extracted from the theory of sense-perception the main idea needed for an understanding of apparitions, I shall say no more about normal sense-perception, but shall leave the reader who wishes to go more deeply into the subject to seek his information elsewhere. The point to bear in mind is that a material thing is composed of two entirely different constituents, (1) a physical object, which is a region of space characterized by certain causal properties, and which exists independently of the observer, and (2) a group, or groups, of sense-data, which are private to the observer and are originated by him. It is with these sense-data alone that the percipient has any direct acquaintance. The sense-data are related in a complicated way to the physical object, but this part of the subject may, for present purposes, be ignored.

Matter is thus a hybrid. It is not something which is just there waiting to be found. It is something which we, during the process of perception, have a hand in constructing.

### 3. THEORY OF APPARITIONS

We are now in possession of the key which explains the nature of apparitions. If the reader will refer back to the specification of the "Perfect Apparition," he will see that what is there described is a material thing without a physical occupant. If we could take a material man and dissolve away his physical constituent without interfering with the sense-data by means of which we perceive him, we should be left with, exactly, an apparition. In a good apparitional case we have all the sense-data which occur in normal perception, but there is no physically occupied region or physical object. Without this physical object there can be no reflected light-waves and no physical sound-waves and no physical pressures on the skin in cases of touch. An apparition lacks physical, causal properties and cannot affect the physical organs of perception. Yet sense-data exactly similar to those which occur in normal perception arise; and not bare sense-data only—complete acts of visual, auditory, and tactual *perception* are built up on the basis of these sense-data. Perception, then, clearly need not be dependent on the operation of physical sense-organs or on any physical processes whatever in the external world. "Hallucinations," which reach the standard of normal percepts in principle, even if they are to some extent imperfect on any given occasion, can be originated by *psychological* factors in the personality. This is an important discovery.

One feature of apparitions shows with particular clearness that not only are apparitional sense-data independent of external, physical causes, but that whatever originates them has power at the same time to control *normally* produced sense-data as well. In the majority of cases apparitions obscure the background. This implies minute and accurate co-ordination between normal and hallucinatory sense-data; for exactly that part of the normal sense-datum which would form the background if the apparition were not there is inhibited to make room for the hallucinatory sense-datum of the apparition. And the same thing happens in the case of apparitions reflected in mirrors. Yet all the while that the background is being inhibited to make room for the apparition, the train of physical and physiological events, which would normally produce the sense-datum forming the background, continues in operation. There must therefore be psychological control of normal perception interfering at some point in what is usually supposed to be a complete psycho-physical causal sequence. Again, some apparitions are transparent, or become transparent before they disappear. In that case there is divided control, the visual sense-datum covering the transparent area being the joint product of the normal visual process and the hallucinatory process, struggling, as it were, with one another.

It seems therefore that sense-data can be originated in two distinct ways: (1) By the normal operation of the physical sense-organs and the physical stimuli they produce in the brain, and (2) by the operation of an *idea,* which, aided by certain mid-level activities in the personality, produces sense-data of exactly the same kind as those which occur in normal perception.

A telepathic apparition may be described, to a first approximation, as an idea received telepathically from an agent and expressed by creating for itself within the percipient's personality the appropriate sense-data. As a rule the idea is that of the agent appearing to the percipient as he would do if present in the flesh; *but any idea can be expressed in this way.* Indeed, a telepathic apparition may, from one point of view, be regarded as a message expressed in the form of a three-dimensional picture. So far this view is not, perhaps, very different from that which has been previously held regarding telepathic apparitions; but it does not seem to have been fully realized hitherto that *the whole apparatus of sense-perception* can be thrown into operation in two distinct ways, (a) from "below" (by normal, physical means), and (b) from "above" (in response to a controlling *idea*). If this dual control be accepted as a fact, it suggests a question about the mode of origination of sense-data. Can they be directly dependent on those physical processes in the brain which are the result of the functioning of the receptor-organs? In normal perception sense-data are supposed to be, at least in part, caused by these processes. This dual control and generation of sense-data suggests that there may be no such direct causation of them by physical processes, but that they may be *psychologically* caused, the physical brain-processes in normal perception playing a guiding and conditioning rather than a causative role; and in the case of hallucinations being possibly dispensed with altogether. The causal agent would be a psychological constituent of the personality whose specialised function it is to produce and control sense-data. This constituent would have to be considered as operating equally in both the cases (a) and (b), but as being set in operation by different means in the two cases. This view, if adopted, in the case of telepathic apparitions would extend to most, if not to all, cases of sensory hallucination, including the small and partial hallucinations which occur in everyday life, those produced in hypnosis, and perhaps those produced by drugs.

I make no attempt to discuss this suggestion from the point of view of normal sense-perception. It raises a large issue and is a matter for philosophers. The only point on which I would say a word is this. How is it, if sense-data are not directly *caused* by the cerebral processes which the receptor-organs produce, that they accompany these processes with such marvellous reliability and precision? First, it may be remembered that events may occur in invariable, or almost invariable, sequence without being casually related. An example of this is provided by the street traffic-lights. When the lights turn red the traffic almost invariably stops; but it does not stop because the redness of the lights *causes* it to do so (that is on any ordinary definition of the meaning of causality). It stops because the redness of the lights acts as a *guide or signal* to the drivers of vehicles, who stop in order to obey the law. Not only is there no cause compelling them to do so; there is interposed the factor of *choice*. An observer so naïve as to interpret the traffic sequence of events as an example of cause and effect might be surprised, if he were out late at night, to discover that there are occasions, in the absence of the police, when the apparently causal sequence is broken.

But, if they are not the result of a cause, how did sense-data ever come to accompany physical brain-processes with such minute and almost unfailing fidelity? I would suggest that this perfection may be due, not to casual efficacy, but to biological necessity. Sense-perception, like all human faculties, is the product of an immensely long period of evolution, and reliability in perception is of vital importance to any animal which is to have a chance of survival. One has only to imagine what would be the effect of an imperfection in perception in the struggle for existence—if, for example, sense-data sometimes failed to come into existence when their physical correlates appeared. What would have happened to a primitive man if the cave bear he was hunting had become invisible for a minute or two? What would happen to ourselves, for that matter, if the traffic were liable to become invisible while we were crossing the road? My suggestion is that the psychological originator of sense-data in the personality has been so well trained in the course of evolution as to obey the physical brain-signals with almost miraculous accuracy. I am not suggesting that this psychological originator exercises actual choice in obeying the signals; only that something occurs which is more *like* choice that it is like mechanical causation. The imperfection and unreliability we find in apparitions would, on this view, occur because the originator of sense-data is there working as an amateur and not as a professional.

This view of the origination of sense-data, it may be said in passing, seems to suggest that a good deal of latitude may possibly exist in the representation of physical objects by means of sense-data. There would appear to be no compelling reason why sense-data should directly convey the characteristics of physical objects. There would be no binding necessity for them to do so. They might be no more than convenient symbols; and it is not impossible that some symbolical scheme of representation of physical objects may have been inherent in sense-perception from the beginning. Once the existence is recognized of elements in the personality endowed with a teleological character, this sort of thing becomes possible.

To return to the apparition, we must regard it, on the present view, as a percept created by this psychological manipulator of sense-data in order to express an idea; or, as I have put it, a percept created from "above." There could be an apparition of anything which the idea happened to contain. If we could take the brick we have used as an example and remove its physical occupant, the result would be that the sense-data by means of which we normally perceived it would disappear, for there would no longer be any light-waves reflected from its surface to affect our eyes, nor any resistance to our hand if we were to try to touch it. Now, if we restored these sense-data by getting the *idea* of a brick to act in a suitable manner on the psychological mid-level constituents of our personality (which I call below the "producer" and the "stage-carpenter," the latter of which has the power of generating sense-data—the hypnotist does something very like this when he says to his subject: You will now see a brick on the table—), we then have an apparition of a brick. The agent of the telepathic apparition does a somewhat similar thing to the hypnotist when he causes a brick to appear as part of the apparition, only he does telepathically what the hypnotist does verbally. There are, I believe, certain differences in the mechanism employed in the two cases, but that may be disregarded for the moment. There is no difference, with regard to the sensory mode of genesis, between the figure of the agent himself, as it appears in an apparitional drama, and the figures of physical objects or animals or of any attendant features which may also appear in it. All are produced in the same way; all are merely expressions of the various factors which the idea contains. There is no need to boggle over the apparition's ghostly garments; they are of the same "stuff" as the ghost itself. Nor is there any need to feel embarrassment, as Gurney seems to have done, when an entire phantom carriage, complete with coachman, footman, and horses appears on the scene. And if the apparition has with it a human companion, that need cause no surprise. All are stage-figures similarly produced. An apparition is a moving picture in three dimensions, and its creator has access to unlimited stage-property. Moreover, he has solved the problem of exhibiting three-dimensional pictures to a collective audience and can allow, down to the minutest detail, for the individual circumstances of each percipient, so that each appears to see the *same* visual solid from his own point of view. This miraculous imitative skill has convinced the world up to now that when an apparition is seen, "somebody is there"; and the rejection of apparitions is largely due to the supposition that they involve this assumption. The mistake is scarcely surprising when one considers how many "proofs" the apparition gives of being present in the ordinary sense—its apparent awareness of its surroundings and appropriate behaviour with regard to them, etc.

When one comes to think of it, the common-sense assumption that a person is "there" when we see him in the flesh is none too easy to justify. What we see is his body and not his conscious self, and all we know about the latter we infer from his body's movements. It is a question whether the statement that his conscious self is "there" really means anything; for to be "there," in the sense of occupying a position in space, means to possess spatial characteristics and to be, for example, so many inches from the corner of the table. But nobody's conscious self can occupy a place in that sense.

The present theory of apparitions throws light on certain puzzling phenomena, such as the Indian Rope Trick.[1] If the evidence for this is trustworthy, the explanation would seem to be that the operator succeeds in instilling the *idea* of the rope and the climbing boy into the personalities of the audience at the right level, much as a hypnotist does, only

[1] See *J*. xi. 299 and *J*. xii. 30. Two phenomena, physical and non-physical, appear to be described. The evidence is not strong.

he does it telepathically instead of verbally. The audience is not hypnotized, neither are the percipients of a collective apparition. The telepathic impulse, if it is powerful enough, seems to be able to "gate-crash" while people are in the normal state. The nearest parallel in the class of experimental apparitions is Wesermann's experiment (Case 44, Ch. V); but the Rope Trick is on a larger scale. Again, if the account of Miss Moberly's and Miss Jourdain's experience in the Gardens of Versailles be accepted, the case does not differ *in principle* from that of a recognized apparition performing some action which was habitual with the recognized person during his life-time. The difference lies in the scale of the environment. Granted that the knowledge was somewhere in existence of what the Gardens were like in 1789, and that somewhere there was an agent (I think this is necessary) to give dynamic force to the *idea* of the Gardens and make it operate on the percipients at the particular time when they were in them, their percipience of the Gardens as conceived in the idea is merely a matter of the accident of their being on the spot when they happened to be *relevant* to the idea as spectators, and that they happened to be sufficiently receptive to react to the idea and give it sensory expression. There is no need, on this view, to invoke retrocognition.

The real question is: How much environment can an apparitional drama contain? There seems to be evidence that it *can* include a complete environment, although it seldom does so. There was a sequel to Case 32 in which Miss Bourne again saw her father on his white horse and saw him in a familiar plantation, but the plantation was invisible from the place where she was standing. It was not until she found that her father had not been in this plantation at all that, she says, "it dawned on me that it was utterly impossible to see either plantation or wall from where I was. Since then I have often been along the same road and looked and wondered how it was I so distinctly saw the broken wall and papa on the white horse; a turn in the road makes my having really done so quite impossible." The environment, as well as the man and the horse, formed part of the apparition. Thus a telepathic apparition may portray almost any idea, and perhaps this fact throws light on certain old legends, such as the metamorphosis of a person into an animal, or the flight of a witch on a broomstick. Anyone who had acquired the art necessary for the performance of the Rope Trick, that is to say the art of producing collective, telepathic hallucinations, could presumably do these things. The creation of hallucinatory sense-imagery, even to a prolific extent, is not in itself a supernormal phenomenon. This fact is, of course, familiar to psychologists and is well illustrated by the following interesting example, which was contributed to the *Proceedings* of the Society for Psychical Research by Mr. John Honeyman, R.S.A.

### 4. A NON-TELEPATHIC, SUBJECTIVE HALLUCINATION

CASE 35   A certain Mr. A. had lost his left eye as the result of an operation for glaucoma, and the sight of his right eye was defective, the central part of the visual field being obscured as if by mist. Apart from this Mr. A. was a perfectly normal person. "In April 1900, Mr. A., walking on a country road, saw on his left a new rubble wall brightly illuminated by the sun, and to his amazement he saw it perfectly distinctly. He could see every separate stone and the mortar joints surrounding it, the smooth faces of the waterworn boulders, and the texture of stones broken to form a face. In particular he was struck with the frequent recurrence of broken granite stones, in which he could distinctly see the hornblende, the felspar, and the quartz and mica reflecting the sun's rays. Indeed, he thought he had never been able to see a wall so minutely before while passing it. He did seem to be passing it quite in a natural way, but presently coming to a part of the road where he knew there was no wall, but only an iron railing on a low parapet, and finding the wall still there and no railing visible, it occurred to him that he might see this wall just as well if he shut his eyes altogether, and on doing so he found this to be the case: the wall was still there, with the sun shining on it as brightly as ever."

Later on the wall disappeared and a variety of other images succeeded it. "These all showed two characteristics, brightness (amounting almost to luminosity) and distinctness—not the slightest trace of haze affecting the natural sight being observable." A favourite image was that of a surface decorated with groups of flowers. The minutest details were distinctly seen. These hallucinations ceased after several days.

About a year later, however, they recurred, this time showing the complete human form. He then saw as distinctly as he had ever seen anything in his life the figure of a female walking so closely in front of him, that he could scarcely avoid treading on her skirt. "The skirt was of red cloth with groups of white lines (a broad line with two very thin lines on each side of it) crossing each other at frequent intervals, as in a tartan, and over this was a black silk jacket or short cloak. The dress was beautifully illuminated with sunlight and moved naturally in response to the motion of the figure, while the light silk jacket was occasionally lifted as if by the breeze." Mr. A. realized that the figure was hallucinatory when told by his companion that no one was there. On crossing to the shady side of the street, Mr. A. still saw the figure with the sun still shining on it. These hallucinations appeared to occupy the visual field of the left eye, which was missing.

This mobile figure, which always kept just out of reach (compare Miss Morton trying to touch her ghost), was accompanied by a more general environment, which was also hallucinatory. "The fields and fences and walls and trees in a landscape seen by Mr. A. as he travelled either slowly on foot or rapidly in a train invariably maintained their proper relationship and perspective, changing their relative positions as the objects in a landscape appear to do." "We have thus," Mr. Honeyman remarks, "one hallucination based on another." His conclusion is interesting. "The truth seems to be," he says, "that subjective visualization is quite independent of physical mechanism, while still in some degree affected by physical conditions."

This case reveals the existence of complete machinery in the personality for producing visual imagery exactly like that of normal perception up to the range of a complete environment, and for making everything appear as natural and as fully detailed as normal sense-perception can do. For this the physical receptor-organs are not necessary. The subject's emphasis on the clearness and minuteness of detail of his visions may be compared with similar emphasis in some of the telepathic hallucinations. One may again recall the case of Miss Moberly and Miss Jourdain in this respect. So far as their finding themselves surrounded by a complete hallucinatory environment is concerned, there is no need even to go to the supernormal for a precedent. The resources of the personality are equal to providing it. The difficulty is, of course, to explain how their environment came to correspond to the Gardens as they were in 1789. The case, if we accept the evidence, bears the marks of being telepathic rather than a subjective reflection of forgotten knowledge of their own.

On the view that hallucinations are expressions of ideas, it is natural to ask what was the idea behind the scenic productions in Mr. A.'s case. It strikes one that his visions were unpurposeful and haphazard, like the pictures of a child amusing himself with a paint-brush. They seem to have aimed chiefly at vividness of colour and design. Possibly some element in Mr. A.'s personality was trying to make up to him for the poverty of his normal vision.

The principle that an apparition is an expression of an idea inevitably leads one to seek for the origin of the idea. Up to this point I have been dealing with the apparition as a sensory phenomenon only. But its sensory expression is only part of the process of its production. There is also the question of how that which is expressed comes into being.

## 5. THE "IDEA-PATTERN"

I have said that an apparition is a percept created to express an idea; but there is evidently a good deal more in it than this. If we revert to a fact, often pointed out as a difficulty against the telepathic theory of apparitions, we shall find that it is more illuminating than appears at first sight; I mean the fact that the agent of an apparition can have no exact or detailed idea in his mind of how he appears to an outsider, yet the apparition represents him in all his details as, in fact, an outsider would see him. When we come to examine carefully the cases forming our evidence, we see that this difficulty is even greater than it appears to be, for the apparition not only exhibits the agent in detail as he would appear to others, but also quite frequently provides him with details or shows him in circumstances of which he cannot have been consciously aware. Subsections (1) to (5) of the section "Imitation of Normal Perception" (pp. 65-72) illustrate this. (1) shows that apparitions behave as if they are aware of their surroundings and conscious of what they are doing. (2), (3), (4) and (5) show that apparitions adapt themselves almost miraculously to the physical conditions of the percipient's surroundings, of which the agent as a rule can know little or nothing. These facts reveal the apparition to be a piece of stage-machinery which the percipient must have a large hand in creating and some of the details for which he must supply—that is to say, an apparition cannot be merely a direct expression of the agent's *idea;* it must be a drama worked out with that idea as its *motif.* It is not easy at first to realize that a figure which opens (apparently) the door of a room and walks in, casts a shadow as it passes in front of the lamp, grows dim as the light fades, is reflected in the mirror, approaches the percipient, looks him full in the face, speaks to him and perhaps actually touches him, is not "there" in the sense in which an ordinary human being is "there." But all the evidence points to the view that what is "there" is only a psychological marionette, the expression of a drama which has been thrown into sensory form, just as the human figures in a film-play are not "there" in the ordinary human sense but are optical constructions contrived to express a drama which has been arranged elsewhere.

It becomes a matter of great interest to ask who constructs these apparitional dramas, and how. We have already caught a glimpse of the machinery employed to express them; but the creation of the drama is a different process. There is evidently a long step between the drama as expressed and the agent's initiating idea. The agent at a moment of crisis certainly does not think of the percipient except in general terms. Probably he does no more than wish to be with him or wish that he could know what is happening to him. His part is only to give direction and impetus to the drama and to supply in very general terms the *motif.* The work of constructing the drama is done in certain regions of the personality which lie below the conscious level; and there the agent's general and simple idea is worked out in complex detail. Simplicity of *motif* and complexity of expression seem to be characteristic of ideas in general. When we have the idea of performing some action, our idea is simple; we do not think of all the complicated movements required to carry it out. These are supplied by some sub-conscious element of our personality. And I rather think that in perception the converse is true, the multiplex detail with which the sense-organs have to deal being unified and integrated into a perceptual idea of sufficient simplicity to be practically useful; although, of course, we can attend to detail if we wish to do so.

Perhaps it would be useful here to introduce a metaphor and to compare the consciousness of the agent to the author of a play, and that "something" within him which works out the idea in dramatic form to the "producer." Further, the "something else" within him which expresses this drama in the sensory form of an apparition may be compared to the "executor" or "stage-carpenter" of the play. These are anthropomorphic terms, but possibly helpful. The author of a telepathic apparition does much less than authors usually have to do. He supplies the most general theme only, leaving a great deal to the originality of the producer. And note that the producer does not exist in his personality alone. The apparitional drama is quite clearly in most cases a joint effort in which the producers of both agent and percipient take part. We know this because not only are there items in the apparition which the agent cannot have known; there are also often items which the percipient cannot have known, such as a wound in a particular part of the body which the agent has received and which the apparition shows, or a coffin or other symbol indicating the agent's death, or perhaps circumstances connected with the agent's accident, such as the appearance of the figure wet and dripping, indicating that the agent has been drowned. Thus the "producers" or "producer-levels" of the agent and percipient must get together to work out apparitions; and in case of collective percipience the "producer-levels" of the additional percipients must also take part. For it is not merely a feat of multiple *perception* which is performed in such cases; it is a feat of *correlation* in which each percipient sees exactly the aspect of the moving apparition which he would see from his particular standpoint in space if the apparition were material. In non-telepathic and non-collective cases only one producer is concerned as in the unshared, but no less marvellously co-ordinated, subjective visions of Mr. A. (Case 35).

It is difficult to picture to oneself the process of construction of such a drama, not only because it takes place beneath the level of consciousness, but also because the processes involved must be very different from anything which takes place in the physical world and different from purely mental processes as well. There is something in it which suggests conscious planning. Yet I do not think that we can imagine that the agent's and percipient's "producers" consciously hold a committee meeting of two and decide on the details of the drama. That is to endow them with too much consciousness. Nor do I think that we can go to the other extreme and suppose that the agent's idea expresses itself through a mechanical pattern which reduces the "producers" to the level of idea-expressing machines. There is a good deal in the apparition which suggests consciousness and there is a good deal which suggests automatism. The truth is that we are dealing with something between the two extremes of consciousness and mechanism. We are dealing with something which is to a certain extent *like* an idea, and, at the same time, to a certain extent *like* a pattern. I have thought it simplest, therefore, to call it an "Idea-pattern." This idea-pattern is the dramatic production of the agent's idea; while the apparition itself is the sensory expression of the idea-pattern. I do not regard an idea-pattern as a substantival entity, but rather as the creative product of substantival constituents belonging to one or more personalities. Perhaps an idea-pattern is related to a "producer" rather as an idea is related to a conscious mind.

An idea-pattern seems to be distinguished by three general characteristics. (1) It is dynamic, for it is usually associated with an initiating drive; (2) It is creative, for it manifests an urge towards expression and completeness; (3) it is teleological, for it is marvellously resourceful in adaptation and in adjusting means to ends. I cannot help remarking here, though it may seem irrelevant, that the character of the idea-pattern suggests strongly the character of countless things in the world of organic life. There is the dynamic will to live or attain expression; there is the creative urge; there is the teleological adjustment, the skill which is neither conscious planning nor mechanical reaction. And there is an inner link between living things which is strongly reminiscent of telepathy, particularly that mutual adaptation which occurs in symbiosis.

If I may digress momentarily in another direction, I would remark that those who maintain a physical theory of telepathy will surely find an additional difficulty in explaining how the agent of a telepathic apparition transmits information which he does not know.

It has been said that the idea-pattern, dramatized by the "producer" and expressed by the "stage-carpenter," is the work of *mid-level* constituents of the personality. It will be as well now to glance briefly at some of the views about mid-level regions which have been discussed in the *Proceedings* of the Society for Psychical Research.

## 6. LEVELS OF THE PERSONALITY

The idea that a human being is not merely a compound of conscious mind and material body but a complex synthesis, composed of many elements which are not necessarily either mind or body, is not new in philosophy. There is the Monadic view of Leibniz; and in recent times psychologists have come to recognize a good deal in the personality which is neither mind nor body. They have postulated an "Unconscious"; and they speak of dispositions and complexes as existent in the personality, thereby implying the existence of substantival constituents of some sort, neither body nor self, but intermediate between the two. But to confine ourselves to views put forward by members of the S.P.R., the conception of the Subliminal Self was early developed by Frederic Myers before, in fact, Freud had penetrated into these regions and announced his theory of the "Unconscious"; and the idea of subliminal entities and activities has been kept in the foreground by the nature of the phenomena we have discovered. The explanation of the mechanism by which script-material is obtained and passed through the levels of the personality to find its final expression in words, developed in connection with the automatic writing of Mrs. Willett, is of particular interest here, for in it we are given, perhaps not with all the lucidity we could wish, but still with logical coherence, a picture of the intra-personal activities involved as they are seen from the communicator's standpoint.[2]

These intra-personal elements of personality were referred to in Presidential Addresses to the S.P.R. by Lord Balfour (1906) and by Professor William McDougall (1920). In the latter the human personality is regarded as an organized and graded hierarchy with consciousness at its head. In such a hierarchy the intermediate members lie between the Self on the one hand and the body on the other, and possess characteristics which are intermediate between those of consciousness and those of matter. I am supposing that those mid-level elements which produce and express an apparition possess some such mid-level characteristics as Professor McDougall suggests.

In the fifth Myers Memorial Lecture, Dr. C. A. Mace outlined a suggestion of what he called a "substantival medium" capable of receiving and re-rendering "patterns of events."[3] He bases this idea on the popular conception of a "psychic ether," or vehicle of "thought-waves," Dr. Mace is very non-committal about the nature of this medium, but I take it that its nature must lie somewhere between the material and the mental. With regard to it he says: "Personally I am of the opinion that we can, with a good scientific conscience, postulate the existence of a medium which records impressions of all sorts of patterns of events, and which later or elsewhere may produce a corresponding pattern. We need not ask: What is the intrinsic constitution of this medium; we need not yet ask how it does it. The postulate medium, in fact, needs only to be endowed with the one virtue expected of all hypothetical entities—the virtue of doing exactly what it is told. In order to be non-committal in respect of what is unimportant I have labelled our hypothetical medium the

[2] See "A Study of the Psychological Aspects of Mrs. Willett's Mediumship," by Lord Balfour in *Proc.* xliii. 41-314.

[3] *Supernormal Faculty and the Structure of the Mind* (1938).

*Tertium Quid,* and I would if I could be even more non-committal still. But however non-committal we may choose to be, we are bound to ask: Under what conditions do these events occur?" Dr. Mace then rendered the conception of this *Tertium Quid* more definite by considering the restrictive conditions under which it might operate, and went on to apply it to telepathy, supposing that an excitement affecting it in one individual might be simultaneously "ecphorized" (a term of Richard Semon's) in another. If I have grasped Dr. Mace's meaning correctly, this *Tertium Quid* is a receptor-vehicle for a complex of engrams of an unspecified nature, and forms a neutral background for the sharing of experience.

Professor H. H. Price suggested in his Presidential Address[4] the possibility that images may exist—"persistent and dynamic entities" he called them, endowed with causal properties —which, once formed, may persist with a kind of independent life of their own. Such images he supposed to be originated by a mental act, but not to be themselves mental. He used them to impart greater definiteness to Dr. Mace's "Psychic Ether" by converting it into an Ether of these persistent images. He then supposed these images, neither mental nor material, to be endowed with telepathic charges and illustrated his theory by applying it to haunting. Such a persistent image might, he suggested, be tied down in some particular way to a physical place or object, might act telepathically on a percipient near this place and might cause him to see an apparition. This image would, it seems, by being itself non-physical while able to occupy physical space, bear a certain resemblance to Myers's "metetherial" occupant of the invaded portion of space. "The apparition," says Professor Price, "might be related to the persisting image in much the same kind of way as the visual sense-datum of a chair is related to a physical chair. For it would certainly be generated by a process in the image (a purely psychical one to be sure, not a psycho-physical one) and it would be located in approximately the same place."

This is a very interesting idea. I find, however, some difficulty in seeing why a purely psychical process of perception, or sensing, should be dependent on the percipient's physical

4 *Proc.* xlv. 307-41.

proximity to the image. The image, itself non-physical, or at most quasi-physical, is anchored by some material influence to a position in space. If it operated *physically* on the percipient's sense-organs, it would, of course, be obvious why he should see the image when he is near the place. But if it operates *psychically* by a process having nothing to do with matter or space, he might surely be expected to see the hallucinatory figure wherever he was. In other words, it seems to me that Professor Price's theory suffers in some degree, like that of Myers, from its hybrid character, being partly physical and partly non-physical.

Such theoretical suggestions and discussions as these are, I believe, of the greatest assistance to our subject. We should freely discuss our material in all its theoretical bearings, since it is on the parallel advance of evidence and theory that progress depends. This is, perhaps, even truer of psychical research than of any other branch of science, for without an advance in theory it may be that no answers are possible to our questions. We are advancing into new territory: we must therefore do our utmost to grasp the new ideas which are to be our chart and compass, and particularly new ideas about the nature of personality. Without these we may merely stultify ourselves by keeping on asking questions which cannot be answered in the old framework. It is important to remember that all questions are asked in terms of some assumed background of thought, and that this background conditions the possible types of answer. Now, it is quite possible —indeed, it is quite likely—that some of the questions we ask are unanswerable in terms of the background of presuppositions that we hold when we ask them. Precognition, for example, may for ever refuse to make sense in terms of a background based on common sense and the experiences of sense-perception. It may be that, through an exploration of human personality, we shall arrive at new ideas about Space and Time in terms of which precognition will make sense. And it is not impossible that the same is true of survival. The paramount importance of gaining new ideas and envolving new theories is therefore clear. Moreover, the hostility to and dislike of psychical phenomena, now so general, appears to rest fundamentally on the fact that they clash with the accepted outlook of the age, which is still, however people may dress it up, based on a fairly crude realism. Hence, to build up theory as we go along is a primary necessity: and in this we need, and are fortunate in receiving, aid from professional philosophers.

Professor Price's interesting Presidential Address offers several tempting leads, which cannot here be followed up. One question, however, almost inevitably arises. Are we to regard Dr. Mace's *Tertium Quid* and Professor Price's "Ether of Images" as quasi-psychological existents subsisting in independence of human beings and forming, as it were, a neutral background, like the psychologist's "Unconscious"? Or are we to regard them as constituents of human personalities? To put it crudely, are Dr. Mace and Professor Price talking about something that is without us or within? If without, is it one universal and neutral background that they have in mind, like the physical world, with which we merely react? If within, does it consist of a number of separate entities which form parts of our personalities? Directly we are faced with something which lies between the material and the mental, we are confronted by the problem of the One and the Many. If an entity has no extended qualities and no spatial boundaries, can it be regarded as being numerically separate from other such entities? Can we say, for example, that although two entities are not spatially separate from one another, they are numerically separate because they possess different contents? Or must we regard all spaceless entities as merging together into a homogeneous block simply because they have no separating space-boundaries? Our mechanistic habits of thought tend to confuse us, for the conception of this block-unity is in reality just as spatial as the conception of atomicity. What we have at the back of our minds when speaking of this block-unity is a homogeneous fluid extended in space; and I suspect that this enters into the idea of a "Common Unconscious." But this is space reintroduced in another guise; for, as Whitehead points out, space has two attributes, a separative attribute and a "prehensive" or holding-together attribute. In the effort we make to get away from space in its separative attribute we come back to space in its prehensive attribute. That is why the formation of new ideas is so important in the investigation of the mid-levels of human personality. In its efforts to grasp the nature of entities which have no spatial characteristics, thought oscillates, baffled, between atomicity on the one hand and homogeneity on the other, both of which are attributes of space. It boggles because we are trying to understand something which has neither characteristic. That is why it has always seemed to me that people who say that the Eastern conception of immortality is that the human soul is "absorbed" into the divine and loses its identity in the process are talking nonsense. They are talking in terms of mechanics. That kind of "absorption" is a property of fluids. When we are speaking of that which has no spatial characteristics, it is difficult to define what we mean by saying that it is *numerically* many: but it is surely equally difficult to define what we mean by saying that it is *numerically* one?

Another way in which habits of thought mislead is that they tend to make us think that individuality, or the character of "I-ness," somehow arises out of the fact of spatial separateness. A pebble on the beach is thought of as being more of an individual than an undifferentiated block of sea-water because it has a visible and tangible surface which enables us to think of it separately and give it a name. Thus, individuality tends to be thought of as arising out of spatial separateness, and we find ourselves thinking that our own individuality arises out of, or is dependent upon, the spatial separateness of our bodies; whereas selfhood is an intrinsic character, irresolvable and not derivative from anything else. Mid-level constituents of the personality reveal a very perplexing thing about this individuality or selfhood. They show this "I-ness" quality, not as something which is either there or not there, but as something which can be present in *degree*. In the personality, the mid-level centres possess in some degree *both* the qualities of selfhood *and* of otherness from self; and it looks as if the higher we go in the personal hierarchy the more selfhood we find and the less otherness. At the head of the hierarchy the pure subject of experience is unthinkable, while the normal self is an enigmatic compound of pure self with the lower personal elements, and by no means a stable compound. We must, I think, look upon our personalities as at once partaking of selfhood and providing an internal environment for self. Even when we come to the lowest level of the personal complex, the body, the same principle holds. I speak of my arm and my coat-sleeve as both being "mine." But there is an intelligible sense in which my arm is "me" as well as "mine." There is, however, no sense in which my coat-sleeve is "me."

In postulating mid-level constituents of the personality, which have no spatial characteristics, I therefore feel entitled to speak of them in the plural with regard to their intra-personal relations. When, as in telepathy, they react with their opposite numbers in other personalities, we may have to think of them in the collective singular. But I should be sorry to say that they *are* either singular or plural. Perhaps when we get away from matter, plurality is also a question of degree. We are in the same sort of quandary over singularity and plurality as the physicists are in over the wave and corpuscular theories of light. For some purposes the wave theory works and has to be regarded as true: for other purposes the corpuscular theory works and has to be regarded as true. But neither theory contains the ultimate truth. We have to make these mental shifts in order to progress.

Professor Price applied his theory of an "Ether of Images" to haunting. The suggestion which I would myself venture to put forward to account for haunting explains the fact that people see ghosts, and explains also the fact that people see both ghosts and crisis-apparitions collectively when and only when they occupy particular positions in space, not by the supposition that their position has any *physical* efficacy, but by the supposition that it renders them *relevant* as spectators to the dramatized theme. Once the spaceless nature of the mid-level elements of the personality is realized, it is seen that their relations with one another must be of a non-spatial kind. There is nothing, then, particularly remarkable in telepathy. It is merely the result of these levels entering into what are, for them, normal relationships with one another. The wonder and the mystery lie in the levels themselves and their extraordinarily interesting character. It is the levels which are "super-normal"; and yet in another sense they are "normal," for they form an essential ingredient in every human being. Probably we coin the term "supernormal" for things which are unfamiliar and commonly hidden from view.

## 7. COLLECTIVE PERCIPIENCE OF APPARITIONS

We are now in a better position to deal with this, the most difficult problem about telepathic apparitions, which has been purposely postponed until this point in the investigation had been reached. Collectivity has been illustrated by Cases 32 and 33. Gurney's explanation was that telepathic percipience is "infectious" and spreads from one person present to another. Myers, on the other hand, thought that the agent in some way "psychically" invaded the place where the apparition was seen and that his "metetherial" presence in space was non-physically perceived by the onlookers. The objections to both theories have been stated

The solution to the problem is, I think, supplied by the "idea-pattern." The maker of the idea-pattern, whom I have metaphorically called the "producer," must be thought of as being linked in the normal way to the other constituents of its own personality by relations of a psychological kind. Normally, it leaves the producers, or producer-levels, of other personalities alone. Perhaps this is not quite true, since experimental telepathy shows that it does not leave them entirely alone. But all cases, whether of experimental or crisis-telepathy, are the result of the producers of two or more persons uniting to form a collective idea-pattern of some sort. Telepathy is no more than the result of a "natural" relationship between the producers of different personalities, and probably they are only doing much the same kind of thing with elements of other personalities that they normally do with their own. The idea-pattern, in the case of a crisis-apparition, which has dynamic power behind it, is a clear and coherent "production" of the idea which existed in germ in the agent's mind. Probably the idea provides the *theme* of the idea-pattern, while the agent's emotional state provides the *drive*. The dramatizing of the idea by the producer is done with a precision, a detail, and a cunning appreciation of the physical circumstances prevailing on the spot which borders on the miraculous (see Ch. II, §3). The key to all the features which are introduced into the scheme is to be sought in the informing *motif*. The commonest theme, of course, resulting from the agent's state of mind at the moment of crisis, is the idea of the agent's own presence in the flesh in the neighbourhood of the percipient. The production of this theme is thorough. The figure is put into all the correct relations with its material surroundings. It is made to appear dim if the light is bad; it is made to be reflected in a mirror if all the angular and other conditions for such a reflection are present, and so on. Whatever would be the behaviour of the physical figure of the agent under existing circumstances is exactly reproduced. This thorough imitation of the physical event, which forms the *motif* of the theme, accounts, I believe, for collective percipience. Other people standing near the place where the apparition is seen would, if the apparition were a flesh-and-blood person, certainly see him. Therefore, to carry out the scheme thoroughly, they are so psychologically acted upon as to see the apparition and to see it appropriately according to their positions and distances. Their "producers" and "stage-carpenters" must, in fact, be got to collaborate with those of the agent and principal percipient. Thus, collective percipience depends on the physical positions of the percipients, *not because physical facts have anything to do with it,* but because their physical positions bring them into the scheme of the idea-pattern. In a word, it may be said that the explanation of collective percipience of apparitions lies not in the "metetherial" presence of a figure in space, as Myers thought, nor in the "infectious" propagation of the telepathic impulse from one percipient to another, as Gurney thought, but in the fact that spectators, by their physical presence, become *relevant* to the theme of the apparitional idea-pattern and, because relevant, are drawn into it.

Since collective percipience of apparitions has considerable theoretical importance, it may be as well to clear the ground with regard to it. In the first place, is the evidence sufficient to make collective percipience reasonably certain? The number of collective cases in the S.P.R. collection is certainly not less than 130, and probably exceeds that figure. This is too large a number to be dismissed out of hand. But suppose it be suggested that in all these cases the narrator alone had the experience but afterwards came to imagine that another person, or persons, had shared his experience at the time. And suppose it be further suggested that in cases where that other person, or persons, contributed their testimony, they shared in this same illusion. We are first met by the fact that all our cases taken as a group are sufficiently accurate to conspire in describing a phantasm of the "Perfect Apparition" type. None has fallen from grace so far as to describe the phantasm of fiction, which performs physical actions. But if the accounts of collective percipience are fictitious, the narrators have fallen very badly from grace in this one particular alone. Is it likely that the narrators would agree in being extremely inaccurate about one feature of their experiences while being accurate about the other features? Take Case 32 as an example. On the assumption we are now making, only one of the two Miss Bournes saw the apparition of Canon Bourne on horseback. The second Miss Bourne and the coachman saw nothing. The coachman's remark that, from the look of the horse, the Canon must have had a nasty accident was never made. All this was added afterwards owing to a hallucination of memory, in which the second Miss Bourne, who signs the joint account, shared. It is most improbable that if only one member of the group of three had seen the apparition, they would all have ridden with one accord in the same direction to see what was the matter. There would have been disagreement and expostulation, and the Miss Bourne who saw the apparition would very likely have started to ride towards it alone. All this, on the above supposition, must have been clean forgotten by both the Miss Bournes in the course of the four years which separated the event from the signed account. The point of real difficulty is that if the testimony of Miss Bourne and of 129 other narrators of collective cases was really as bad as this, these cases must be worthless as a whole. Must one not suppose that narrators who suffered from such glaring lapses of memory where the question of collectivity was concerned suffered from it also where other points in their experiences were concerned? The answer to this is that, if they imagined the whole of their experiences, they would never have succeeded in describing the "Perfect Apparition." And since the "Perfect Apparition" proves that they were substantially accurate in describing their experiences as a whole, it seems fantastic to suppose they fell into gross inaccuracy on the one point of collectivity only.

Or take Case 30. If the narrator had been the only person who saw the phantasmal carriage coming down the road, there would not have been such general astonishment at its non-arrival, or at the subsequent arrival of the real carriage. The others would have said that the narrator had made a mistake and a discussion would have ensued, the whole of which must, on the above view, have been afterwards forgotten; while the story of the arrival of the daughter, saying that her father and mother had driven past her on the road without speaking, must have been a pure invention. One other point should be noticed. In collective cases it is frequently reported that one, or some, of those present do not see or hear the apparition while the others do. Now this is evidence supporting the non-physical character of the apparition, and falls into line with the non-collective cases; so that, if the statements about collective percipience are untrue, we must suppose that, even in their worst lapses, the narrators have still remained true to their ideal of describing the non-physical ghost. If they invented collective percipience, it would surely have been more natural to say that *all* the additional percipients saw or heard the apparition.

In case after case the same difficulty meets us, and there are cases of haunted houses in which either the apparition has been collectively seen or heard or else we must discredit the evidence wholesale. (See particularly Case 16.) My own conclusion is that the collective percipience of apparitions must be accepted, or else the spontaneous evidence must be rejected altogether.

If collective percipience be accepted, it appears to constitute a proof of telepathy, provided the conclusions reached above about the various theories of apparitions are valid. So far as I am aware, only three explanations of the collective percipience of apparitions have been put forward: (1) that the apparition is a physical object and is seen, heard, and felt by means of the physical receptor-organs of the body in the course of normal perception; (2) that an apparition occupies space in a "metetherial" but not in a physical sense, and that it is collectively perceived without the aid of the physical sense-organs because it is a public and neutral, though non-physical, object; (3) that an apparition is not a physical phenomenon but a sensory hallucination, and is collectively perceived because of some kind of telepathic process taking place between the percipients. The objections to the first two explanations have been already pointed out. The second is very vague and seems to involve the contradictory view that physical space is also non-physical. Some form of the third view seems to me to be inevitable. I am suggesting that the "telepathy" which accounts for collective percipience is the establishment of a relationship between the mid-level centres of the personalities of the percipients of such a kind that it causes each to play his part in expressing a collective idea-pattern. It is, in fact, only an extension of a similar relationship connecting the personalities of agent and principal percipient. If we could succeed in producing collective percipience experimentally, we might find out a good deal about telepathy.

As has been said before, an idea-pattern cannot be regarded as the result of a consciously held committee meeting of two or more producers; nor can it be compared with a physical field having its focus in space at the place where the apparition is seen. There is a certain amount of analogy with both these; something on the one hand which resembles skilful planning, for it is not as though a fixed picture, like a photograph, appeared on a wall: the apparition is a moving picture, astonishingly adapted to fit the physical conditions. But, on the other hand, it can be looked at from an external point of view, and the percipients regarded as behaving like factors in a *pattern*. Whatever position they take up in space, they sense the sense-data appropriate to their position, just as wherever a compass-needle is placed in a magnetic field, it points in an appropriate direction. We are dealing with something between an *idea* and a *pattern*.

Of course the realization of these idea-patterns is very imperfect. Often some of the persons present do not see the apparition or only see it imperfectly, or only hear it while others see it, and so on. It may be that it is not easy for the agent's producer to get at other people's producers and induce them to enter into the game; or it may be that the executive members of potential percipients sometimes fail to give expression to the idea-pattern by producing no sense-data.

There is one feature which suggests divided allegiance on the part of the executor or "stage-carpenter," namely the occasional transparency of the apparition. The background is then seen through the apparition, which means that the sense-datum is partly the result of action from "above" and partly the result of action from "below." The stage-carpenter is trying to play two parts at once.

It looks as if collective percipience were a peculiarity of telepathic apparitions. There is no evidence, so far as I am aware, that purely subjective hallucinations spread to others. Gurney quotes as subjective hallucinations certain collective post-mortem appearances, but, as he himself admits, we cannot be sure that these are subjective. The notable case supplied by Mr. Honeyman (Case 35) was pretty clearly subjective, and no mention is made of anyone having shared Mr. A.'s visual experiences. Neither do hypnotic sensory hallucinations appear to be shared; but this field has never been exhaustively explored from the point of view of psychical research. Much useful work might be done, for example, in endeavouring to induce collective hallucinations under hypnosis, using two or more subjects, and possibly searching for subjects of the right type. It may be that in this direction lies the best hope for bringing extra-sensory perception under experimental control.

With regard to the subject of haunting, in which the ghost is seen collectively, I would suggest that collective percipience here is brought about in the same way as with crisis-apparitions. Given that a dramatic idea-pattern is formed, the features it contains will be provided on account of their relevance to the theme. In collective percipience, people who are near the apparition are caused to see it because their physical situation makes them *relevant* as percipients. Similarly, the idea-pattern constituting a haunting ghost has for its theme a figure moving about in a particular house or locality. Anyone in this house or near this locality becomes a relevant percipient and is psychically operated upon so as to become one. There is really no difference in this respect between the ghost and the crisis-apparition. The crisis-apparition, during the brief period of its existence, "haunts" the place where it is seen just as the ghost does, and is seen there (circumstances permitting) by anyone who happens to be in the neighbour-hood. The difference is that the crisis-apparition chooses to "haunt" the place where the desired percipient happens to be. The ghost chooses to haunt a place on other grounds, and if it is seen or heard while it is doing so, that is incidental and arises from the fact that people have placed themselves ap-propriately to enter into the theme of its drama. Similarly, the fact that a ghost goes on haunting a place, while a crisis-apparition "haunts" it only once, is the result of the different intentions animating the two themes. It is not that ghosts and crisis-apparitions are two different types of phenomenon: it is that their idea-patterns differ in content.

If this view of ghosts and haunting is correct, it implies that the ghost is a telepathic phenomenon originated by some agent. In some instances, such as Case 52, the evidence points to a living person on the spot as being the agent. In others, it is hard to find a plausible candidate for the agency other than a deceased person. The possibility of mixed agency must not be overlooked.

## Chapter IV

## "Clairvoyance"

### 1. RECIPROCAL APPARITIONS

SOME OF THE MOST difficult cases from the theoretical stand-point, which occur amongst apparitions, are those called "reciprocal." In these both parties have a simultaneous ex-perience. The number of such cases is small; but they are very instructive. The following is a typical reciprocal case which brings out the theoretical problems involved.

CASE 36   Mr. S. R. Wilmot, an American, was crossing the Atlantic in 1863, returning home in company with a friend, a Mr. W. J. Tait, who shared his cabin. The cabin was right aft, and, owing to the slope of the ship's side, the two berths were not vertically over one another. Mr. Wilmot occupied the lower berth and Mr. Tait the upper.

After eight days of bad weather, Mr. Wilmot was enjoying his first night of refreshing sleep, when, as he says, "towards morning I dreamt that I saw my wife, whom I had left in the United States, come to the door of my state-room, clad in her night-dress. At the door she seemed to discover that I was not the only occupant of the room, hesitated a little, then advanced to my side, stooped down and kissed me and after gently caressing me for a few moments, quietly withdrew. Upon waking up I was surprised to see my fellow passenger . . . leaning upon his elbow and looking fixedly at me. 'You're a pretty fellow,' said he at length, 'to have a lady come and visit in this way.' I pressed him for an explanation . . . [and] at length [he] related what he had seen while wide awake, lying in his berth. It exactly corresponded with my dream."

The narrator says that, on arriving home and meeting his wife, "almost her first question when we were alone together was, 'Did you receive a visit from me a week ago Tuesday?' 'A visit from you?' said I. 'We were more than a thousand miles at sea.' 'I know it,' she replied, 'but it seemed to me that I visited you.' 'It would be impossible,' said I. 'Tell me what makes you think so.' My wife then told me that on account of the severity of the weather and the reported loss of the *Africa* . . . she had been extremely anxious about me. On the night previous, the same night when . . . the storm had just begun to abate, she had lain awake for a long time thinking of me, and about four o'clock in the morning it seemed to her that she went out to seek me. Crossing the wide and stormy sea, she came at length to a low, black steamship, whose side she went up and then descended into the cabin, passed through it to the stern until she came to my state-room. 'Tell me,' she said, 'do they ever have staterooms like the one I saw where the upper berth extends further back than the under one? A man was in the upper berth looking right at me, and for a moment I was afraid to go in, but soon I went up to the side of your berth, bent down and kissed you and embraced you and then went away.'" Mr. Wilmot's wife and sister add their testimony in confirmation of the report.

It may, I think, be doubted whether Mr. Wilmot's experience was, properly speaking, a dream.

At first sight this case seems to afford strong evidence in support of Myers's view that a consciously observing mind is present in space where the apparition is seen; for Mrs. Wilmot remembered the experience of having been in the cabin, and having seen the interior from a point of view in the doorway, where her apparition was seen to stand; she also remembered the arrangement of the berths, the presence of a man in the upper one, and her hesitation on entering. Mrs. Sidgwick, however, commenting on the case, says that she still adheres to Gurney's telepathic view. She does not think that Mrs. Wilmot could have seen *any* cabin in the way she saw this one; that is to say she regards her seeing the cabin as due to a telepathic link with her husband—a telepathic effect for which he, as agent, was responsible. She compares this case with the Paquet case (Case 12). Mrs. Paquet, like Mrs. Wilmot, saw the agent in his actual surroundings; but she saw the tragedy some six hours after it had happened and can scarcely, therefore, be supposed to have been undergoing the experience of being psychically present on the spot when it occurred. If the Paquet case was telepathic, why not the Wilmot case also? The sharing of the experience by Mr. Tait would, on Gurney's view, be explained by his having acquired it "infectiously."

Now, it was pointed out in Ch. II, §1 that apparitions can appear in different kinds of space. Disregarding minor variations, one may say roughly that they appear: (i) in the physical space of the percipient's own surroundings; or (ii) in a special space of their own, such as in a disc apparently cut out of the opposite wall, or a figure on the polished surface of the wardrobe, or a scene appearing in a sheet of glass, or in a crystal, etc., or even in a dream; or (iii) the percipient may seem to be transported into the agent's actual surroundings. Mrs. Wilmot's was an instance of (iii). Mrs. Paquet's was half-way between (ii) and (iii). Messrs. Wilmot's and Tait's experience was (i)—if we agree that Mr. Wilmot was not really dreaming.

Case (iii) is identical with what has been called "travelling clairvoyance," and the problems set are these. (a) In case (i), is the agent and generator of the apparition actually present in some valid sense where the apparition is seen? (b) In case (iii), is the percipient and "clairvoyant" experient actually present in some valid sense at a point in space from which he views that scene? I have answered question (a) in the negative, having regarded the apparition as an elaborate sensory construct created by mid-level elements of the personalities of agent and percipient working together, and not as a conscious or semi-conscious being. I now suggest that question (b) must also be answered in the negative, and that a similar piece of elaborate constructional work goes on in this case also, which results in the apparition being seen, not in the percipient's own surroundings, but in the agent's surroundings. The resources of the mid-level constructors are evidently immense, and the material for constructing the distant scene, which the clairvoyant perceives, can usually (if not always) be obtained from the minds of some persons or other. It must be remembered that the agent of an apparition is not consciously aware of his own personal appearance; yet he appears with all the details which an observer would see. In the case of distant clairvoyance, why should not the details of the distant scene be worked up into a picture by a similar eclectic process? There is evidence in these phenomena of immense skill in the staging of sensory constructs. This is a sign of their importance. One cannot reflect too much on the almost miraculous constructive powers of these mid-level centres.

It seems to me, therefore, that Gurney and Mrs. Sidgwick, rather than Myers, are on the right track in the explanation of reciprocal cases. But I should not say that Mrs. Wilmot's experience of voyaging across the sea to her husband's ship and finding her way to his cabin, etc., was just a telepathic message sent to her by him. I would rather say that it was an apparitional drama constructed by the mid-levels of both their personalities working in collaboration. Also, I would not say that Mr. Wilmot's experience, which was the result of a second apparitional drama, constructed in a similar way, spread to Mr. Tait by "infection." I would say that Mr. Tait was drawn into the scene because his presence in the cabin rendered him relevant as a spectator. *His* mid-level factor was acted upon because the play would not have been complete without him. The play in case (i) is, of course, to make the apparition appear in every way as much like a normal human being as possible and to supply every detail to make it complete.

## 2. "TRAVELLING CLAIRVOYANCE"

As has been said, crisis-cases of type (iii) are closely similar to cases of so-called "travelling clairvoyance"; and some examples of the latter must now be quoted. They lie midway between the spontaneous and experimental fields. The kind of subjects who see these distant scenes appear to possess a spontaneous, trance-like state, which is at the same time capable of being controlled. They should be invaluable for experimental work in extra-sensory perception.

CASE 37   Such a subject was "Jane," the wife of a Durham pitman, for whose case Myers collected the evidence. "She never received any fee," he writes, "or made any exhibition of her powers." Jane appears to have fallen spontaneously into a peculiar kind of trance in which she was able to answer questions put to her. On one occasion Dr. F., the operator, told a patient of his, a Mr. Eglinton, that he would try the experiment of getting Jane to visit him clairvoyantly between 8 and 10 p.m., and Mr. Eglinton said he would be in a particular room at the time. He was very thin from the effects of an illness, and at the appointed time Jane, in trance, was led in thought to the house by verbal direction and guided to the right room. She then said she saw the door opening, and a very fat man with a corporation and a cork leg coming in, and sitting down at the table with papers beside him and a glass of brandy and water at his side. Asked if she could see his name on any of the letters about, she said Yes; and spelt it correctly—Eglinton.

Dr. F. thought her description of the man completely wrong, but found afterwards that Mr. Eglinton had wished to try an experiment and had had his clothes stuffed with pillows to represent a very fat figure and placed at the table, on which were papers and a glass of brandy and water.

The experiment is instructive on account of its mistakes as well as on account of its successful features. The information about the appearance of the figure could have been obtained from Mr. Eglinton's knowledge, but so could the fact that it was a dummy. Yet the sensitive does not appear to realize that the figure is a dummy. She combines a true account of the figure's appearance with her own assumption that it is a living man, and adds the untrue detail that it opens the door and comes into the room. In the false imputation of a cork leg to the figure there seems to be a half suspicion that there is something artificial about it.

Now, as the account is presented (and as, in fact, all similar accounts of scenes are presented by clairvoyants), the whole scene—the figure seated at the table, the papers, the brandy and water, and the entire interior of the room—is described as if seen from a particular point in space, and gives the impression that the clairvoyant is standing in the room and looking round exactly as a person materially present in the room would do. I suggest that this is an elaborate piece of dramatization, and that the clairvoyant is not present as an observer in space at all. The whole scene described by the clairvoyant is a dramatic construct worked out by the mid-level producer of the clairvoyant's personality in conjunction with the producers of other persons who possess the relevant information. These producers, in fact, create an idea-pattern between them, which is given sensory expression by the executor or stage-carpenter belonging to the clairvoyant's personality. In the construction of this idea-pattern, some of the items are taken from knowledge possessed by other persons, which is telepathically acquired, and some is supplied by the clairvoyant's own ideas and expectations. All the sense-data composing the scene are correlated with astonishing skill to present this scene as viewed from a particular point in space, the *motif* being to imitate as closely as possible the scene that would be presented to a person materially present at that point. In this, I think, we have the analogue of the apparition, but turned, so to speak, the other way about. In the case of the apparition, the place in space is chosen at which the apparition is to appear, and the mid-level constructors get to work to produce the necessary idea-pattern and to correlate the sense-data so that the percipient shall see the apparition at this spot. In the case of so-called "clairvoyance," the idea-pattern in constructed so that the apparition shall be seen *from a place* instead of *at a place*.

There seems, therefore, to be nothing in these "clairvoyant" cases which compels us to assume that the clairvoyant "travels" or is consciously present at a point of observation in space, as Myers supposed. I am not even sure that the statement that a consciousness is present at a particular point in space has any meaning. Anything which occupied a position in physical space must surely itself possess spatial properties, that is to say it must be spatially extended. For the meaning of saying that a thing occupies a particular position in space is that it is so many feet or inches away from another thing which occupies another position in space. And how can a consciousness be so many inches away from, say, the corner of the table? The statement is clearly nonsense. When we, as material persons, say that we are looking at the interior of a room from a particular position in space, we mean that our *bodies,* and particularly our eyes in the case of visual observation, occupy a definable position in that room. We can say just how many inches our eyes are from the corner of the table. But our *consciousness* does not occupy the position of our eyes. To say that it does so is to talk nonsense. Our perceptual consciousness has constructed for it an elaborate system of sense-data, which gives it a picture of a spatial environment as seen *from* a particular standpoint, and gives it an irresistible feeling of *being in* that picture. And that, after all, is not so dissimilar from what goes on in the case of apparitions and clairvoyance. Sense-data are immaterial entities and their relation to physical objects is of a most complex kind. Normal sense-perception,[1] as well as supernormal, depends on works of construction almost miraculous in their complexity and subtlety. The specious simplicity thrown over

[1] See H. H. Price, *Perception,* ch. ix.

sense-perception by common sense is a sheer piece of illusion, provided by Nature for reasons of practical utility. Just as the specious simplicity of the conviction that one's consciousness is present at a point in space, held by everyone in practical life, is exploded on close examination, so it is with most of the things which appear obvious to common sense. They turn out on examination to be pieces of fiction instilled into us by Nature because they are practically useful. "Materialism," as it is called, or rather miscalled, is the unthinking attitude which accepts these illusions naïvely. It is, in fact, the outlook of those who have failed to see through Nature's devices.

The importance of studying cases of apparitions and clairvoyance is that these cases throw light on what is happening beneath the surface in the depths of the personality.

CASE 38 Another group of clairvoyant cases was reported by Dr. Alfred Backman of Kalmar, in Sweden. He experimented chiefly with a subject, rather similar to Jane, called Alma. On one occasion, without anything being prearranged, he told Alma to go to the Director-General of Pilotage at Stockholm and see if he was at home. She described him as sitting at the table in his study, writing. Among other things she saw a bunch of keys on the table, and she was sharply ordered to seize these and shake them and to put her hand on the Director-General's shoulder. This she repeated two or three times until at last Alma declared that he observed her. On being told of the experiment subsequently, the Director-General's account of his own experience was as follows. "On that occasion," he said, "he was sitting, fully occupied with his work, when, without any reason whatever, his eyes fell on the bunch of keys, lying near him on the table. He then began to consider how he could have put the bunch of keys there, and why it was there, when he knew for certain that he was never in the habit of leaving it there. While reflecting on this, he caught a glimpse of a woman. Thinking it was his own maid-servant, he attached no importance to it, but when the occurrence was repeated, he called her and got up to see what was the matter. But he found nobody, and was informed that neither his servant nor any other woman had been in the room. He did not, however, observe any rattling of the bunch of keys or of any movement of the keys."

These are merely examples to illustrate the kind of thing that has been called "travelling clairvoyance." The reader who is interested will find a number of similar cases on record. The evidence for this kind of phenomenon cannot be lightly dismissed, for it receives support from the results of careful experiments carried out on quantitative lines, which, however, lie outside the scope of the present survey. So far as Backman's experiments are concerned, it is worth while to notice that he was visited at Kalmar in 1890 by Professor Richet, M. Houdaille, Dr. A. T. Myers, and Frederic Myers. "Perhaps the most important outcome of our visit," says Myers, "was the conviction we all of us gained as to the absolute candour and disinterested desire for truth with which Dr. Backman's experiments are conducted, and the simplicity and good faith of the subjects whom he employs."

This experiment appears to contain a hint that if "travelling clairvoyance" were given sufficient dynamic power, it would pass over into the class of apparitions. It would become, however, an apparition of the rare class in which the agent remembers the distant scene in which he has appeared, and becomes comparable with the experience of Mrs. Wilmot (p. 128). Dr. Backman appears to have imparted a good deal of energy into the orders given to Alma. He "sharply ordered" her two or three times to seize the keys and to attract the Director-General's attention, and, under these circumstances, the latter saw a fleeting apparition of the sensitive. Had the urge been still stronger, he might have seen the keys lifted off the table by the apparition, although, of course, the physical keys would still have remained where they were. So that in the case of "travelling clairvoyance" the subject's producer-level dramatizes the distant scene for him, and there the matter stops. In the more powerful case of the reciprocal apparition, the producer-level of the person who is present at the spot clairvoyantly visited is drawn into the idea-pattern as well, and his reciprocal part in the drama is staged in addition.

The question whether, in cases of clairvoyance, the subject ever gets to know facts which could not be obtained from *any* mind is debatable—and also important. If the evidence for precognition be admitted, it is not sufficient to show that the fact clairvoyantly cognized is known to no other mind at the time. It is also necessary to show that it *never will be known* to any other mind. Further, if retrocognition be a fact, it is also necessary to show that it *never has been known* to any other mind. These are usually impossible conditions to fulfil, because the fact cognized has to be known to some one in order to be verified.

CASE 39 The case in which M. Ossowiecki read, in Poland, with extraordinary accuracy and under unimpeachable conditions, the contents of a sealed envelope which had been prepared with the greatest care in London, is often cited as evidence for clairvoyance. But of course the contents of the envelope were known to the person who had prepared it, and so telepathy is quite capable of explaining the incident.

CASE 40 Some experiments were made by Dr. A. T. Wiltse of Skiddy, Kansas, on a subject called Fannie G. In one case a well-known man, "Uncle Julian Scott," had ridden into the Emerald River and been drowned and his body had not been found. Fannie appears to have located his saddle under a tree at the bottom of the river, where it was afterwards found. But the evidence is not quite clear; and in any case, if the position of the saddle were afterwards known to those who found it, it might have been a case of precognition.

It is clear that the statements of clairvoyant subjects are not infrequently wrong, and the sensory scenes they witness are no doubt partly built up from their own expectations.

In experimental telepathy, or extra-sensory perception, the same kind of thing probably happens as in the case of the "travelling clairvoyant" subject, but in experimental telepathy, as commonly carried out, the effects are much weaker, because ordinary people, and not especially good subjects, are chosen as percipients. Mass experiments in telepathy appear to show that there is sufficient looseness in the mid-level constituents of ordinary people's personalities for cross-relations among these mid-levels to take place and reveal themselves, provided a sufficiently sensitive method is employed for detecting them. But the sensory constructs obtained under these conditions are of a very vague and wandering kind.

### 3. "PURE CLAIRVOYANCE"

The question whether such a thing as *pure* clairvoyance, in the strictest sense, is possible possesses a good deal of theoretical interest; for pure clairvoyance is only another name for direct perception of physical objects without the aid of normal sense-perception. As has been pointed out, we know physical objects only through the intermediary of our own sense-data, and these sense-data we ourselves create. *By no normal process can we achieve a state of direct awareness of a physical object;* so that if there is such a thing as pure clairvoyance, it is our *only* possible means of becoming *directly* acquainted with the physical world. When once a sense-datum belonging to a physical object has been sensed by a living mind, we cannot assume that an extra-sensory subject, who manifests knowledge of that object, has obtained it by pure clairvoyance. Nor can we if any sense-datum belonging to the object ever *will* be sensed by a living mind, on account of precognition. Similarly, of course, the possibility of inferential knowledge must be ruled out. It becomes an interesting question to ask whether an experiment can be devised to test if such a thing as pure clairvoyance is possible.

In 1936 the writer published an account[2] of an apparatus designed to test extra-sensory perception by the use of a restricted system of choices, the success above chance expectation being estimated statistically. The essence of the method was as follows. Five small boxes with close-fitting spring lids were placed in a row before the subject to be tested. Each box contained a small electric lamp, and the lamps were lit, one at a time, by a mechanical method in an unknown but strictly random order. The subject at each trial attempted to open the box with the lighted lamp in it, there being no possible clues for normal sense-perception to act on. The trials, the successes, and the failures were recorded by automatic apparatus, and, with the knowledge that the expectation of chance-success was one in five, the successes in excess of chance could be easily obtained. Now, it seems as if this apparatus

[2] *Proc.* xliv. 99-166.

might afford a means of testing pure clairvoyance. It is, in fact, a case in which the quantitative method has an advantage. The lighting of an electric lamp is an event in the physical world. Let us be clear about this. The bright glow of the filament, which we see when we look at a lighted electric lamp, is *not* an event in the physical world. It is a visual sense-datum, which we ourselves have created, and a sense-datum is not a physical event. The warm feeling we experience when we touch the bulb is *not* an event in the physical world either. It is the objective counterpart of a sensation; that is, it also is a sense-datum. The *physical* event is a change in the causal properties of the filament, the bulb, and the surrounding space, whether we picture this in terms of the motion of electrons or of the generation of electro-magnetic energy. *The filament of the lamp is not shining brightly inside the closed box, nor is the bulb of the lamp warm.* Both filament and bulb are manifesting *different physical causal properties* when the lamp is, as we say, "alight" from those they are manifesting when it is not alight: that is all. When we say that the lamp *is* bright and hot inside the closed box, we mean that *if we* could get inside the box we should see it as bright and feel it as warm. That being the situation, we want to know whether it is possible for anyone to become aware of the special physical properties of the lamp when it is alight without the assistance of any of the sense-data which normally make us aware of those properties. This is the strict meaning of "clairvoyance." But the conditions are more stringent still. In view of the possibilities of precognition, it will be necessary to make sure that no one *ever will be* aware of which lamp was alight when a success was scored, and that this lighting of the lamp never *will* have any sense-data belonging to it.

These conditions are not easy to comply with; but I believe that with the help of this apparatus it could be done. Let us suppose that the results of the experiments are recorded on two automatic electric counters, one counter giving the total number of trials and the other the total number of successes scored. The means for doing this already exist. The counters would have to be kept covered and out of earshot until the end of the experiment. The lamps in the boxes would, in addition, each have to be placed in a permanent light-tight case inside its box, so that on opening a box the subject would not know whether it was alight or not. The operator does not in any case know which lamp is alight on any occasion, since his duty is merely to operate a switch which starts and stops a revolving selector, which he cannot see, and which lights the lamps mechanically one at a time at random. No one therefore knows, or ever will know, which lamp was alight when a success or a failure was scored. The physical event is a lighting-occasion, *and no actual sense-data belonging to any lighting-occasion will ever have existed.*

In order to test whether any clairvoyant faculty has been at work, it is only necessary to read the two counters at the end of the experiment, which give the total number of trials and the number of successes. By applying the standard formula, it can easily be calculated whether the successes are significantly above the number which chance would provide.

I suggest this as a theoretically possible method for testing clairvoyance or, in other words, for testing whether a human being can be directly cognizant of the physical world. There may be other methods of carrying out the experiment, and, if so, it is to be hoped that experimenters will try them. I rather fear that the experiment is likely to be less satisfactory in practice than in theory, for it is, in a sense, an attempt to prove a negative. If the experiment failed, even on a large number of occasions, it would scarcely be safe to conclude that it had failed because the feat was impossible. It might well fail for other reasons.

4. SUMMARY OF TYPES OF SENSORY HALLUCINATION

It may be useful at this point to sum up the different kinds of hallucinatory phenomena which, it is suggested, probably fall under the present general theory.

A. *Telepathic apparitions*

Under this heading I include not only the fully externalized kind, but also those which present themselves in special kinds of space, or are seen in crystals, etc., or in cases of so-called "travelling clairvoyance." This type also includes the faint images seen by percipients in experimental telepathy—images which are probably the joint product of telepathic influence, imagination, and memory. I say nothing here of the hallucinations experienced by entranced mediums, since these do not come within my present terms of reference; but on the face of it these appear to present analogies with telepathic apparitions.

## B. *Common, partial hallucinations*

The hallucination in these cases, which occur in everyday life, embodies some idea well fixed by habit and inserts it, expressed in the form of a sense-datum, into a normal percept. The suggestion I would venture to put forward is that such ideas have, in the mid-level regions of the personality, corresponding idea-patterns; and that these idea-patterns are sometimes able to capture the psychological machinery (normally under the control of the receptor-organs and their neural accessories) which generates and arranges sense-data, and by this means to express themselves in sensory form. Such idea-patterns might of course be called psychological "traces," but the term "trace" scarcely conveys the essential character of an event in a mid-level factor of the personality, namely, that it lies midway between an idea and a pattern or trace.

## C. *Sensory hallucinations produced under hypnosis*

I make no claim to any detailed knowledge of these hallucinations, which form a separate branch of inquiry. Subject to correction, which facts revealed by a detailed study of hypnosis might entail, I suggest that, so far as the internal processes occurring in the percipient are concerned, the hypnotic hallucination is similar to the telepathic hallucination, the main difference being that in the hypnotic case the idea, of which the hallucination is the expression, is verbally suggested by the hypnotist; whereas in the telepathic case the idea is derived telepathically from the agent. But this statement is not quite correct, for it is not the agent's *idea* which the percipient telepathically receives. The situation is that agent and percipient together, working in the mid-level regions of their personalities, jointly create the idea-pattern, which finds expression in the percipient's executive level, or which, metaphorically, is staged by the percipient's "stage-carpenter." I conceive, therefore, that a joint idea-pattern is constructed in the telepathic case (that is what constitutes telepathy) and that an idea-pattern is constructed singly in the hypnotic case, sensory expression being attained by similar mechanism in both cases. One striking difference between the telepathic hallucination and the hypnotic hallucination is that the former tends to be collective (about one third of the cases in which more than one person is present are collective), whereas the latter (so far as I am aware) does not. I can suggest no reason why hypnotic and, indeed, purely subjective hallucinations also do not spread to bystanders, whereas telepathic hallucinations, in a certain proportion of cases, do. We are very much in the dark concerning the structure of human personality, which is probably far more extensive and complex than at present we have any idea of; and it may be that the telepathic process taps a factor in the personality which the hypnotic and subjective processes leave untouched.

D. *Dreams and purely subjective hallucinations*

These seem to be the results of idea-patterns formed, not to express conscious ideas, but to express such things as complexes, hopes, fears, etc., formed in the personality or to express states of health or physical conditions. They show that dramatic idea-patterns need not owe their origin to conscious ideation. Indeed, a few apparitional cases show the same thing, as when the apparition of a living person, who is unconscious that anything is happening, is seen from time to time, and the process appears to be congenital to that person, the apparition being accompanied by no crisis.

E. *Hallucinations produced by drugs and anaesthetics*

Here the first cause is definitely physical; but I do not see that it follows that the immediate cause of the hallucination need be physical. Physical processes in the brain may be concerned in exerting a *guiding* influence, as in the case of other types of hallucination, but not necessarily a *causal* influence.

The hallucinatory flashes, sounds, tastes, and smells which occur when the receptor-organs are directly stimulated, as by a blow on the eye or an electric current, are, I would suggest, originated in quite a different way from the other hallucinations, being a distorted form of normal sensation.

## Chapter V

## Agency of Apparitions

### 1. THE AGENCY BEHIND AN "IDEA-PATTERN"

HITHERTO THE IDEA-PATTERN has been considered chiefly in connection with crisis-cases, where the agency is obvious, the pattern embodying the agent's wish or idea at the moment. But there are other cases in which it is not so clear how the idea-pattern originates or whence comes the informing idea. The subjective hallucinations of Mr. A. (Case 35), are a case in point. There are also cases in which we can be fairly certain that no conscious idea, or at best only the feeblest conscious idea, led to the formation of the idea-pattern. There are people whose apparitions seem to stray about while they know nothing about it—people who in Myers's phrase possess the faculty of "psychorrhagic diathesis." Presumably there exists some kind of subconscious wish to be elsewhere; and the mechanism which enables such a wish to find expression may be more easily set in motion with these people than with the majority. In Case 30 we are told that the pair who were seen in the carriage had no intention of starting "till Mr. Robert Coe, suddenly starting from his chair, exclaimed, 'Let's go to Clement's.'" This apparently initiated the apparition. There are other cases in which the sudden idea of being at a place seems to have been the cause of the agent's appearance there. There are cases on record in which percipients have seen apparitions of themselves. I do not think we need regard these as involving any new principle, since any figure can appear in an apparition. No doubt it is rare for a person to be agent and percipient at once; but there are some reciprocal cases in which this double role is played.

## 2. CASES OF SELF-APPEARANCE

CASE 41  Here is a case of self-appearance. The percipient and her husband had a married cousin and her husband staying with them. "One night when we were having supper," she says, "an apparition stood at the end of the sideboard. We four sat at the dining-table; and yet with great inconsistency I stood as this ghostly visitor again in a spotted light muslin summer dress and without any terrible peculiarities of air and manner. We all four saw it, my husband having attracted our attention to it, saying 'It is Sarah' in a tone of recognition, meaning me. It at once disappeared. None of us felt any fear, it seemed too natural and familiar."

An appended note adds: "The dress in which the figure appeared was not like any that Mrs. Hall had at the time, though she wore one like it nearly two years afterwards." She had had certain other hallucinations, which makes it appear probable that she herself was the agent in this one.

A point arises in this case which it is worth while to deal with here. It has often been pointed out by the collectors of these cases (and the loophole is eagerly seized by those who wish to explain the evidence away), that when one member of a party sees an apparition and makes some remark or exclamation about it, this acts as a suggestion, which causes the others to see the apparition too. But a little reflection will show that this process cannot be at all general; that, in fact, if it ever occurs at all, it must be very rare. Otherwise it would only be necessary to say, "Look there!" or "There is so-and-so!" for the person addressed to see an apparition. If this sort of thing really happened the world would become peopled with apparitions to such an extent that one would never be sure who were the living people. Indian Rope Tricks would be as common as blackberries, and the interesting possibilities open to schoolboys and others would not for long be overlooked. As it is, we have evidence that universal suggestibility of this kind does not exist. An example of this was given in Case 2. Again, the sequel to Case 26 was, we are told, that "the young ladies looked out for the apparition on the same night the following year but saw nothing." In another case[1] the percipient, who had had two previous experiences of an apparition in a certain house, went to stay there again later. Although she "half expected to see the old lady," the narrative continues, "she saw and heard nothing whatever." In Case 16 Miss Morton says: "We were all on the look out for her that evening, but saw nothing; in fact, whenever we had made arrangements to watch, and were especially expecting her, we never saw anything." It looks as though expectancy had an inhibiting rather than an encouraging effect on the seeing of apparitions.

CASE 42   In 1929 Archbishop Frederic (E. J. Lloyd) wrote to Sir Oliver Lodge, saying that on the 14th of January he arrived home feeling very tired, sat down and fell into a deep sleep, from which, however, he continues, "I was sharply aroused in about a quarter of an hour (as I perceived by the clock). As I awoke I saw an apparition, luminous, vaporous, wonderfully real of myself, looking interestedly and delightedly at myself. Some books lying on a table back of my ghost I could see and identify. After I and myself had looked at each other for the space of about five seconds, my ghostly self vanished for a few seconds, only to return in a more definitely clear way, but for a few seconds only."

CASE 43   It has been pointed out to me that Goethe once had the experience of seeing himself as an apparition. It was when he was leaving Frederika at Strasburg and riding away on horseback. "When I held out my hand to her from my horse," he says, "the tears were in her eyes, and I felt sad at heart. As I rode away along the footpath at Drusenheim a strange phantasy took hold of me. I saw in my mind's eye my own figure riding towards me attired in a dress I had never worn—pike grey with gold lace. I shook off the phantasy, but eight years afterwards I found myself on the very road going to visit Frederika, and that, too, in the very dress I had seen myself in, in this phantasm, although my wearing

[1] *Proc.* xxxiii. 384.

it was quite accidental." It is not quite clear from the account whether the figure he saw was fully externalized in space.

In the majority of cases in which the apparition is of a person who is undergoing no crisis at the time, it seems probable that the person is himself the agent and that his appearance is due to some temporary or permanent peculiarity in the state of his personality. I would suggest that that constituent of the personality which I have called the "producer" then relaxes for the time being its normal relationship with the other constituents of its own personality, and becomes more ready to enter into relationship with the personalities of others. With some people this tendency may be congenital. Such was probably the case with Canon Bourne (Case 32), who was twice seen when nothing was happening to him.

CASE 44  One of the experimental cases reveals a significant fact. It shows that the figure appearing in a telepathic apparition need not be that of the agent, a feature, I think, which might be expected when one realizes that an apparition is only a mode of conveying a message, which may consist of anything. The case is quoted in *Phantasms of the Living* (I, p. 10), but a fuller and more evidential account is given in a small German book, *Der Magnetismus und die Allgemeine Weltsprache,* published in 1822 by H. M. Wesermann, who was Government Assessor and Chief Inspector of Roads at Düsseldorf at that time.

Wesermann, the agent, had been in the habit of trying experimentally to make his own apparition visible to people. This time he varied the procedure by trying to make the percipient see the apparition of some one else. The account proceeds: "A lady who had been dead five years was to appear to Lieutenant —n in a dream at 10:30 p.m. and incite him to good deeds. At half-past ten, contrary to expectation, Herr —n had not gone to bed but was discussing the French campaign with his friend Lieutenant S— in the ante-room. Suddenly the door of the room opened, the lady entered dressed in white, with a black kerchief and uncovered head, greeted S—with her hand three times in a friendly manner; then turned to —n, nodded to him and returned again through the doorway."

We have the first-hand account of Lieutenant S—, one of

the two percipients, which is as follows. He says that Herr —n had come to spend the night at his lodgings. "After supper," he continues, "and when we were both undressed, I was sitting on my bed and Herr —n was standing by the door of the next room on the point also of going to bed. This was about half-past ten. We were speaking partly about indifferent subjects and partly about the events of the French campaign. Suddenly the door out of the kitchen opened without a sound, and a lady entered, very pale, taller than Herr —n, about five foot four inches in height, strong and broad in figure, dressed in white, but with a large black kerchief which reached to below the waist. She entered with bare head, greeted me with the hand three times in complimentary fashion, turned to the left towards Herr —n, and waved her hand to him three times; after which the figure quietly, and again without any creaking of the door, went out. We followed at once in order to discover whether there were any deception, but found nothing. The strangest thing was this, that our night-watch of two men, whom I had shortly before found on the watch, were now asleep, though at my first call they were on the alert, and that the door of the room, which always opens with a good deal of noise, did not make the slightest sound when opened by the figure."

Wesermann speaks as if such cases as these were not often successful, and states his belief that they can only be produced when the agent is in a very emotional and excited state and when the percipient is specially susceptible. It is, of course, not at all likely that the dead woman had anything to do with the apparition. The case is on a par with other experimental cases in which the agent caused his own figure to appear to the percipient; but in this case the theme was varied, and the figure of another person appeared instead.

There are two interesting points about this case. In the first place the apparition was more than an expression of the agent's conscious idea. It gives clear evidence of the creation of an idea-pattern; for Wesermann did not know there were two percipients present. He thought Lieutenant —n was alone and in bed, and must have imagined the apparition approaching him in his bedroom. The whole drama of the appearance in the ante-room instead of in the bedroom, and the separate greeting of the two percipients, must have been the joint work of the agent's and percipients' producers. Secondly, the case shows that the person represented by the apparition need not be the agent. If an apparition represents a dead person, therefore, this is not sufficient proof that the dead person is the agent. A living agent *can* produce it. On the other hand, the consensus of evidence goes to show that this kind of apparition must be produced by *some* agent; and in the majority of cases it is hard to find a plausible candidate other than the person the apparition represents.

Apparitions, as has been said, fall into the four classes: (1) Experimentally produced apparitions; (2) Crisis-apparitions; (3) Recognized apparitions of persons some considerable time dead (Gurney arbitrarily places the limit of time separating these from Crisis-apparitions at 12 hours after death); (4) Ghosts habitually haunting places. There is no reasonable doubt about the agency of the first two classes. In (1) it is obviously the person who is trying to make his apparition visible at the time when it is seen. In (2) it is just as obviously the person who is undergoing the crisis, whether this be death or some other event. In every case that I have come across in these two classes, except the Wesermann case quoted above, the agent has himself been the centre of the apparitional drama, whatever else may have been present in the drama as well.

Gurney interpreted these two classes of cases as "phantasms of the living"; and where, in the second class, the crisis was death, he included as phantasms of the living all cases in which the phantasm appeared up to 12 hours after death, regarding these slightly post-mortem appearances as due to deferred telepathy. The percipient had, he thought, subconsciously received the telepathic message from the agent at, or before, the moment of death, but it had lain dormant for a time. Myers, on the other hand, regarded the agent as being "metetherially" present in space where the apparition was seen. If Myers was correct in his view, all the cases which Gurney put down to deferred telepathy would evidently form strong evidence for survival; for the agency is not in doubt, and the agent is, on Myers's view, in some good sense actually present on the spot. The view advanced in these pages rejects

Myers's interpretation, while it radically alters Gurney's. It is of interest to ask whether, if this present view be accepted, it is compatible with Gurney's view of deferred telepathy. I think in a sense it is; but, if deferment occurs, I should expect it to do so because it forms part of the theme constituting the idea-pattern. In practice there does not as a rule appear to be any evidence that the agent wishes to be with the percipient at some period *after* the crisis he is undergoing. On the contrary, there is more often an urgent desire to be with the percipient at the time. It is, of course, possible that deferment might occur during the process of expression by the percipient, without forming part of the theme of the idea-pattern. But since the percipient carries out the sensory expression of the idea-pattern, and does so with extraordinary fidelity to the theme, this seems rather unlikely. The independent evidence for the deferment of telepathic impulses advanced by Gurney does not seem to be very strong, resting as it does mainly on the deferment of tastes, etc., observed during telepathic experiments. In crisis-cases the sense of urgency might be expected to militate against deferment.

### 3. POWERFUL EFFECT OF SOME CRISIS-CASES

The theory of deferment, as Gurney puts it forward, suggests the idea of a faint telepathic impulse being picked up by the percipient and lying dormant in his subconscious region until he goes to bed, or enters a quiet state, when it works its way to the surface. But that is not at all the sort of thing which seems to happen in a number of crisis-cases, although it is possible that it happens sometimes. The telepathic impulse does not behave at all gently: on the contrary, it crashes in like a thunderbolt. This is the kind of thing one reads. I "rushed down to the drawing-room again, and, sinking on my knees by my husband's side, fainted and it was with difficulty I was restored to myself again."[2] Again, the percipient burst into tears when asked about her experience and said, "I suppose I fainted, as I lost all recollection for some time, and when I came to myself the apparition had gone—but of one thing I am sure, and that is *that it was not a dream.*"[3] "It made

2 *P.L.* (312).                      3 *P.L.* (313).

such an impression on my mind I shall never forget it."[4]
"The following circumstance is impressed upon my mind in
a manner which will preclude its ever being forgotten by me
or the members of the family interested."[5] "It is nearly thirty
years ago now, but it is as vividly impressed on her memory
as if it had happened yesterday."[6] "I only know I shall never
forget it."[7] "She was terribly frightened, rushed into a neigh-
bour's house and dropped in the passage."[8] "I turned round
and saw my husband's mother, looking very death-like. I said,
'Oh mother, what a start you gave me!' But she was gone. A
feeling of great depression came over me, and I was quite
unable to go on my husband's errand, but went home. . . . I
fainted before I saw Mr. Alger and after recovering, I felt
unwell so that I had to go to bed."[9] Then again there is the
case of Lord Brougham, when travelling in Sweden. He had
made a schoolboy pact with a friend (whose existence he had
now almost forgotten), that whichever died first should appear to the other. He was lying comfortably in a warm bath,
when, he says, "on the chair sat G., looking calmly at me.
How I got out of the bath I know not, but on recovering
my senses I found myself sprawling on the floor."[10] "So suddenly did I spring up out of my heavy sleep that I nearly
knocked my head against the berth that was over mine."[11]
"My cries alarmed the whole family, who came crowding
into the room."[12] "She was much alarmed by sounds of great
distress from her mistress, which led her hastily to ring for
assistance and summon her master, for her mistress's weeping
and agitation were uncontrollable. As soon as her husband
entered the room, Mrs. Williams exclaimed, 'Susan is dead.
She has been to take leave of me.' "[13] "We each thought the
other was taken ill, and turned in alarm. . . ."[14] "These things,
when they occur, take a deep hold on us, and although it
happened more than 52 years ago, we both of us remember
it as freshly as if it were but a year ago." Compare also the
experimental case in which the agent said of Miss V., the
percipient, "She had seen me so vividly in her room (while

[4] P.L. (341).       [8] P.L. (257).       [12] P.L. (512).
[5] P.L. (352).       [9] Proc. v. 294.     [13] P.L. (628).
[6] J. vi. 27.        [10] P.L. (146).      [14] P.L. (678).
[7] P.L. (210).       [11] P.L. (507).

widely awake) that her nerves had been much shaken and she had been obliged to send for the doctor in the morning."[15]

One feels that it would be futile to say to these percipients, "You must have dreamt it!" One has also some doubts about the theory that these powerful telepathic impulses are deferred until the percipient is in a passive state before they emerge.

There is another point about these cases which invites a short digression. If it is suggested that they coincided with their crisis-events by chance, the question is raised as to whether there is a class of cases in which powerful effects of this kind are experienced, but which do not coincide with any corresponding event. If there are, I have not come across them; if there are not, the suggestion that they coincided by chance seems to have no meaning. For chance can only deal with a class of homogeneous events. If some members of the class hit the mark while others did not, there is a basis for estimating how likely it is that those which hit did so by chance. But if *all* the members of the class hit the mark, then there is no meaning in saying that they did so by chance. If, to provide a class for a statistical calculation, we take events of another kind and mix them with the events we are interested in (say we take unimpressive waking visions of quite another kind which coincided with no external events) and treat them all together as if they were one class, then we may get a probability figure, but it will be merely misleading. This is one of the dangers of quantitative methods when applied to psychical research.

## 4. AGENCY OF POST-MORTEM CASES

Gurney's explanation of Class (3), the post-mortem cases, is that they are purely subjective. They occur too long after death to be reasonably attributed to deferred telepathy from the living; nor do they coincide with any crisis-event which might point to their being telepathic. One difficulty for the subjective explanation is that these post-mortem cases are sometimes collective. So far as I am aware (although I cannot claim to have made any thorough investigation of this

15 *P.L.* 16.

field), those hallucinations which we have best reason to regard as purely subjective are never collective; so that collectivity would seem to be a sign that the case is in one way or another telepathic. In Case 35 the subject, Mr. A., had many subjective hallucinations extending over a considerable period of time, and on account of his bad sight he must have been constantly attended by others; but no mention is made of any of his hallucinations having been shared. Some cases, coming under Class (3), certainly contain some evidence for the view that the deceased person represented by the apparition is actually the agent.

CASE 45    For example, some people had taken lodgings on the first floor of a house while an invalid lady occupied the ground floor. This lady died suddenly one day, and the next night the percipient awoke to see, standing at the foot of her bed, "an old gentleman with a round, rosy face, smiling, his hat in his hand, dressed in an old-fashioned coat (blue) with brass buttons, light waistcoat and trousers. The longer I looked at him," she says, "the more distinctly I saw every feature and particular of his dress, etc." She described the apparition next day to her niece, who was astonished and said she had exactly described Dr. R., the husband of the deceased lady, who had died three years before. The difficulties of putting this case down as purely subjective are obvious. In the first place the percipient had never seen or heard of the person she described. In the second it is not quite true to say that the apparition coincided with no external event. It coincided with Mrs. R.'s death. If the agent was not the deceased Dr. R., it must have been Mrs. R. before she died, and the telepathic impression must have been deferred. There is usually some way of evading a survivalist explanation; but I think if we are candid we must admit that, as the cases mount up, these explanations have the air of being rather a ragged set of makeshifts, and that a good many cases, regarded apart from *a priori* considerations, do point to a surviving agency.

CASE 46    Two ladies were looking over a church in which was placed the tomb of an old friend of one of their families. This friend had left a sum of money to have glass put into a window in his memory, but his heir had neglected his wish On hearing this story, the narrator of the case says that she

felt quite angry and said to her companion: "If I was Dr. —
I should come back and throw stones at it." "Just then," she
continues, "I saw an old gentleman behind us, but thinking he
was looking over the church took no notice. But my friend
got very white and said, 'Come away, there *is* Dr. — !" Not
being a believer in apparitions, I simply for the moment
thought she was crazy. . . . But when I moved, still looking
at him, and the figure before my very eyes vanished, I had to
give in." Here again the collective feature has to be explained
if it is maintained that the hallucination was subjective.

CASE 47   An old lady (Aunt Harriet) was very ill and was
being nursed at night by a relative, Mrs. John Pearson, in a
front room. In the back room, with the door wide open and
the landing lighted, were Mrs. Coppinger and the narrator.
The account continues, "About 1 or 2 a.m. . . . both Mrs.
Coppinger and myself started up in bed; we were neither
of us sleeping, as we were watching every sound from the
next room. We saw some one pass the door, short, wrapped
up in an old shawl, a wig with three curls at each side and
a black cap. Mrs. Coppinger called out, 'Emma, get up, it is
old Aunt Ann.' I said, 'So it is, then Aunt Harriet will die
to-day." We jumped up, and Mrs. John Pearson came rushing
out of the room and said, "That was old Aunt Ann. Where
is she gone to?" I said to soothe her, "Perhaps it was Eliza
come down to see how her mistress is." Mrs. Coppinger ran
upstairs and found Eliza sleeping in the servant's room. . . .
Every room was searched, no one was there, and from that
day to this no explanation has ever been given of this appearance except that it was old Aunt Ann come to call her sister,
and she died at 6 p.m." This case is again collective.

CASE 48   There is the case of an American commercial
traveller who, while engaged in making out orders and smok-
ing a cigar, suddenly saw the apparition of his dead sister
close to him. She looked perfectly natural except for a red
scratch on the right cheek. When, later, he mentioned this
fact to his mother, she nearly fainted and told him that she
had accidentally made just such a scratch on his sister's body
before burial, but had immediately effaced it with powder
and had told no one. The mother died a few weeks later so

that the apparition, by appearing when it did, enabled the fact of the scratch to be verified by the mother's account.

There are also cases in which knowledge of things has been brought to light by apparitions, such as the Chaffin Will case[16] and a case in which an apparition revealed the presence of money sewn up in a coat.[17] I will not, however, stop to quote these.

CASE 49 The evidence of young children for what they claim to have seen is probably as a rule not very reliable. But when it is a case of the entire behaviour rather than of the words of a child the case is different. In this case a child had died at the age of eight months, and his little brother, aged two years and seven months, said to his mother every day after this, "Mamma, baby calls Ray." He would leave his play to say this, and wake his mother at night to tell her, saying, "He wants Ray to come where he is; you must not cry when Ray goes . . ." "One day . . . he came running as fast as he could run, through the dining-room where stood the table with baby's high chair (which Ray now used) at the side. I never saw him so excited, and he grabbed my dress and pulled me to the dining-room door, jerked it open, saying, 'Oh, Mamma, Mamma, come quick; baby is sitting in his high chair' As soon as he opened the door and looked at the chair he said, 'Oh, Mamma, why didn't you hurry; now he is gone. . . .'" The child, who had been perfectly well, was taken ill and died nine weeks after his brother. These seem to be remarkable hallucinations for a normal child of two and a half.

CASE 50 The Bowyer-Bower case is an interesting one, for four people had visual hallucinations of him at different times. The evidence was collected by Mr. Hubert Wales. Eldred Bowyer-Bower, aged 22, was an airman and was shot down and killed early in the morning of March 19, 1917. On the same day, and within 12 hours of his death, his apparition was seen by his half-sister in India, to whom it appeared so real that she thought at first he was there in the flesh. She turned to put her baby down in a safe place, and, turning back, held out her hand to him, but he was not there. She did as everybody does on these occasions, called and

16 *Proc.* xxxvi. 517.                    17 *Proc.* viii. 200.

looked everywhere, and only gradually was it borne in upon her that she had seen an apparition. About the date of the death and before the fact was known, his sister's child of nearly three (in England) came into her mother's room and said, "Uncle Alley Boy is downstairs." On the same day, March 19, before the fact of the death was known, a friend of the family wrote saying that she was in a state of great anxiety over Eldred. In December 1917, some nine months later, the airman's fiancée awoke and saw his apparition sitting on the bed beside her. She spoke to him and records that "His lips started to move," and he made a reply "just above a whisper." She tried to touch the apparition but her hand went through it. In November or early December 1917 the airman's mother had an interesting experience. During the night she came over first very hot and then very cold. A yellow-blue ray shot across the room and moved till it was in front of her. As she watched it she says, "Something like a crumpled filmy piece of chiffon unfolded and the beautiful, wavy top of Eldred's head appeared. A few seconds and his forehead and broad beautiful brow appeared, still it waited and his lovely blue eyes came, but no mischievous twinkle, but a great intensity. It all shook and quivered, then his tiny little moustache and mouth. I put out my hand and said: 'Eldred, I see you,' and it all flickered quite out, light and all." Small recurrences of the ray occurred and slight feelings of cold. The percipient says that she got no more sleep and is satisfied it was not a dream. Of course the child's evidence can be dismissed and the appearances after the death was known assumed to have been subjective hallucinations; but this seems rather thin, for the experience of the airman's mother bears all the marks of being a telepathic experience. Note the mode of appearance of the head of the apparition, which is closely paralleled in an experimental case reported in the S.P.R. *Journal* (vii, 250).

There are several features about these post-mortem cases, therefore, which make it difficult to account for them as subjective hallucinations.

When unrecognized apparitions are seen once and never again, the subjective explanation is easier. But even here we come up against the difficulty that some of them are collective, as, for example, Case 26.

The agency of Class (4), ghosts, presents a difficult problem. Some ghosts are recognized as being like former inhabitants of the houses they haunt; others are not.

CASE 51 It may be as well to take one of the best observed and best authenticated ghost-cases on record, that of the "Morton" ghost, already quoted in another connection as Case 16, and note its chief features. Miss R. C. Morton (pseudonym), a medical student, evidently had, from the way she reports her researches, a well-balanced, scientific mind and was free from superstitious fears. She, as well as the principal observers in the case, were personally interviewed by Frederic Myers.

(i) The hauntings lasted for seven years, from 1882 to 1889.

(ii) During this period about twenty people heard the ghost and of these at least seven saw it; probably more.

(iii) the hauntings rose to a peak period in 1885, and after 1886 gradually faded away.

(iv) The figure was usually taken for a real person by those who saw it for the first time.

(v) All the observers agreed as to the description of the figure, which was tall, wearing a dark dress with widow's weeds, with one hand usually half hidden in the folds and a handkerchief held to the face. One observer did not see the handkerchief. The face was never well seen, but the general description tallied with the appearance and habits of Mrs. S., the second wife of a former tenant.

(vi) The house dated from about 1860 and had only been occupied by two families before the Morton family, and their history was known.

(vii) The phenomena consisted of the visual apparition, which followed, more or less, a routine, going down the stairs from the bedroom landing to the drawing-room, standing at a particular spot in the bow-window, then leaving the drawing-room by the door, going along the passage and disappearing by the garden door. Also footsteps were heard by many percipients always of the same description. "Her footstep is very light," says Miss Morton, "you can hardly hear it except on the linoleum, and then only like a person walking softly with thin boots on." The swish of woollen drapery was also heard. These footsteps were unlike any of those of the Morton family. All the servants were changed during the period of the hauntings; but the footsteps went on unaltered. There were other sounds, especially during the peak period, of bumps, turning of door-handles, heavy and irregular footsteps, heavy thuds and bumpings, noises like heavy articles, such as boots, being thrown across the passage, and the sound of something heavy being dragged.

(viii) The sounds were sometimes collectively perceived, as many as five persons having heard them at once. The visual apparition never seems to have been actually seen by more than one person at a time; but it was on one occasion seen by the four Miss Mortons in quick succession in four consecutive positions on its route from the drawing-room to the orchard.

(ix) Besides the evidence of awareness of its situation provided by the behaviour of the figure, in walking up and down stairs, through doorways and along passages, etc. (Miss Morton once saw the figure deliberately walk round her father, who could not see it), on more than one occasion it stopped and looked as if about to speak when Miss Morton addressed it.

(x) The non-physical character of the figure was proved in several ways. It appeared in a room with the doors shut; it vanished while being watched; it was twice seen to pass through threads lightly fastened across the stairs; it became less substantial and solid-looking towards the end of the period. It is obvious that no *physical* sounds could be caused by the feet of a figure having no substantiality; for sound-waves are caused only by the reaction on one another of physical bodies. Miss Morton's frequent attempts to touch the figure failed because it always managed to place its visible surface beyond her reach. Sometimes one person would see the figure while another present would not. Miss Morton's father never saw it, although she pointed out to him the place where she saw it and he went and stood by it. It then moved round him.

(xi) The figure had no luminosity of its own, and behaved

with reference to the lighting of the scene as a material figure would have done.

(xii) Cold feelings, or a cold wind, sometimes accompanied the figure.

(xiii) The dogs were affected by the apparition. A retriever was several times found in the kitchen in a state of terror. A skye terrier twice ran to the foot of the stairs, wagging its tail at an invisible something, and jumping up and fawning. Then it suddenly slunk away with its tail between its legs and ran under a sofa.

(xiv) Miss Morton says, "I felt conscious of a feeling of *loss* as if I had lost power to the figure." Also some mental connection between the figure and the percipients is indicated by the fact that "the figure has not been called up by desire to see it, for on every occasion when we had made special arrangements to watch for it, we never saw it. On several occasions we have sat up at night hoping to see it, but in vain—my father with my brother-in-law, myself and a friend three or four times, an aunt and myself twice, and my sisters with friends more than once; but on none of these occasions was anything seen. Nor have the appearances been seen after we have been talking or thinking much of the figure."

What agency are we to attribute to such a ghost as this? My own suggestion is that the ghost is essentially the same phenomenon as the crisis-apparition, the post-mortem apparition, and the experimentally produced apparition. All four cases consist of idea-patterns produced by mid-level "producers" in the personalities of the percipients, and in the case of crisis and experimental apparitions by the personalities of the living agents as well. The differences between these three phenomena lie in the differences between the *themes* of their idea-patterns. Now, the idea-pattern constituting the Morton ghost must have been in part the contribution of the producers belonging to Miss Morton and the other percipients. But these cannot have originated the theme any more than the percipient originates the theme in a crisis-case. We must look for an agent who is capable of producing the theme. I must confess that I cannot see any plausible agent other than the surviving self or personality of the Mrs. S. whose appearance and habits the ghost reproduced.

We might, of course, point to the Wesermann case (Case 44), and say that this proves it possible for the agent of an apparition to be quite a different person from the individual whom the apparition represents. This is quite true; but Wesermann deliberately tried to make the apparition be that of a particular person he had in mind. If the Morton ghost were a similar phenomenon, some unknown living agent, who had known Mrs. S. in life, must have been deliberately trying, night after night, for seven years to cause Mrs. S.'s apparition to appear in the house, carrying on this practice as a kind of gigantic and long drawn-out hoax! The effort would have been prodigious, and the explanation is surely quite unplausible.

A ghost appears to be similar to a crisis-apparition or any other apparition except that its idea-pattern has a different theme. The theme of the crisis-apparition is usually inspired by a desire on the agent's part to visit his friend, so the drama which is worked out is that of the agent in his friend's vicinity trying to communicate with him. The ghostly theme is different, being that of brooding reminiscence. The ghostly drama is therefore that of the agent's figure performing long familiar actions in a familiar place. Little or no notice is taken of persons who may happen to be about the house because they form no part of the theme. The fact that a crisis-apparition appears only once while a ghost keeps on appearing is also accounted for by the different content of the two themes. In one way, however, people who happen to be in the haunted house *are* drawn into the ghostly idea-pattern.[18] They are relevant to the pattern as casual observers. They are drawn in and psychologically operated upon so as to see the relevant sights and hear the relevant sounds simply because all cases of these telepathic idea-patterns imitate a material scene (that is their *motif*) with great exactness and insist on including observers if these have so placed themselves as to be relevant. I therefore explain the fact that people who happen to be present in a haunted house see and hear the ghost in the same way as I explain the fact that people who happen to be on the spot when someone

[18] They are not relevant to the theme itself but they are relevant to the circumstances in which the theme is dramatized.

sees a crisis-apparition, see it too. In both cases the seeing and hearing is fluky and uncertain, depending on the psychological make-up of the percipient. In neither case is it due to anything physical.

But there are other types of haunting, which suggest that the agency is to be looked for in another direction.

CASE 52 The following case was investigated by Sir William Barrett, F.R.S., in 1914. The haunting occurred in an old house in Worcestershire, inhabited by a Mr. and Mrs. Roberts and their family. To begin with, the housemaid, tidying a bedroom, heard groans coming from under the bed, saw a figure emerge from it and then heard footsteps passing round the room and going out of the door. Another maid heard footsteps. The nurse heard a tremendous noise in the night coming from the room below, as if the windows were being pushed up and down; and the next night was frightened by groans coming from the cook's room overhead. The cook had heard nothing, but complained of noises in her room from time to time. Again, the nurse, described as a cool-headed woman, "woke suddenly one night, then heard footsteps come into the room and walk in a great hurry between her bed and my elder little boy's, felt something brush past her head, then heard the footsteps hurry to the dressing-table, then back and cease at the door. During this time, and while the noise was still in the room, she managed to strike a light, but there was nothing to be seen. . . . A few nights later the same thing occurred, but that she had a feeling of a hand being put on her throat, and of receiving a push." A noise was heard like that of an iron bedstead being kicked. "My husband," says Mrs. Roberts, "has since had much the same experience, accompanied by a feeling of great stupor. He attributes it to indigestion!" This sort of thing continued erratically for some time, terrifying the domestic staff, until presently it was suspected that the cook had something to do with it. She admitted that something of the kind had happened in houses where she had been before. But it is clear from the account that the cook, who is described as "not young," could not possibly have done it by playing tricks, for when a light was lit in a room where the sounds were still going on, it revealed nothing; and on one occasion the housemaid felt herself pushed in one of the bedrooms and rushed downstairs to the kitchen, where she found the cook dishing up the dinner.

Although the phenomena were of the poltergeist type, the evidence tends to show that they were non-physical. In the end the cook left, and Mrs. Roberts wrote, "Since Mrs. E. (the cook) has gone on the 12th inst., we have had 'peace, perfect peace' as far as ghosts are concerned."

I think in a case like this one must suppose an idea-pattern to have formed itself in the cook's personality uninformed by any intelligent idea, but informed only by some dissociated fragment. It is, however, an idea-pattern of the telepathic type, since it pulls relevantly placed percipients into its scheme if they are sensitive enough. There is no need to look beyond the cook for the agency. The Morton ghost was quite different. It will be remembered that it went on just the same after all the servants had been changed. But there, too, unintelligent noises developed during its peak period; and it may be that some cases of haunting are complex, being partly the reminiscent type of ghost of a deceased person and partly the poltergeistic type originated by some living person on the spot. Possibly the one type stimulates the other in some way.

## 5. RELATION OF GHOSTS TO CRISIS-APPARITIONS

There is no clear line of demarcation between ghosts and crisis-apparitions, a few cases being intermediate; and this makes it difficult to suppose that the ghost is a totally different phenomenon from the crisis-apparition.

CASE 53 The family in this case consisted of Dr. and Mrs. S., their son, who had lately lost his wife, and their daughter with her family, consisting of a son, a daughter, R., aged 23, another, E., aged 20, another, C., aged 19, and a fourth, A., a year or two younger; the principal witnesses were interviewed by Sir Oliver Lodge.

The apparition was taken to be that of the son's dead wife, and was first seen collectively by C., A., and a friend Miss G., soon after she died. Not long afterwards it was again seen collectively by A. and Miss G. Then by a cousin and a servant, and then by R., who saw the apparition of her aunt repeatedly. It was generally seen near the bedroom and dressing-room of Mr. S., the widower. The appearances continued for nearly a year and a half, and then Mr. S. married again and left the house, when the appearances ceased. Some five months later he returned on a visit, and "the children again fancied they saw their aunt."

It seems here that the ghost haunts the house, like an ordinary ghost, yet the haunting centres about a person, as with a crisis-apparition.

CASE 54 "A young couple were engaged. Her father withdrew his consent, the mother on her death-bed made its renewal her last request. The father, instead of getting over his sorrow, seemed more and more bowed down with an ever-increasing sense of 'horror.' One day he told his married daughter and her husband that his wife haunted him every morning at 4, the hour when she died, always talking of the young couple. They asked him what clothes the apparition wore, and he said, 'The last dress I gave, and a cap of your making.' On the way home the married daughter told her husband that it was when in that dress and cap that her mother had said to her, 'If I die before your father renews his consent, I shall haunt him till he does.' She was then in perfect health. This was never told to the father, but he was urged to renew his consent. For some months he could only escape the visitations by having some one *awake* with him in the room. From the day he consented again to the marriage his wife's visits ceased."

This certainly sounds rather like the traditional ghost-story; but Mrs. Sidgwick personally interviewed the narrator, the other married daughter.

CASE 55 General Sir Arthur Becher, who held a Staff appointment in India, took a house in Kussowlie for the hot season. On the first night he awoke suddenly and saw the figure of a native woman standing near his bed. He got up and followed the figure, which retreated into the bathroom and disappeared. The outer door of the bathroom was locked. A few days later, Lady Becher saw standing close by her and in the bathroom a native woman, who disappeared by the same door as before, which was locked. The same night their youngest son, aged eight, started up in bed and called out, "What do you want, ayah?" evidently seeing a female figure in the dressing-room. The family lived in the house for months afterwards, but the figure was not seen again. They learned from other occupants that the figure was a frequent apparition on the first night or so of the house being occupied: a Cashmere woman was said to have been murdered by the door leading into the bathroom. Here the haunting has reference to the occupants of the house as well as to the house itself.

Case 6 provides an instance of a ghost of the ordinary haunting type, which nevertheless takes a certain amount of notice of the inhabitants of the house, looking at them, in one instance slapping a percipient on the back, and speaking (a thing which crisis-apparitions not infrequently do but ghosts very seldom do), saying in a sorrowful voice, "I can't find it."

CASE 56 A family leased a house in West Brompton for seven years, and for the first eighteen months nothing happened. After that a grey figure was seen about the house, and was seen repeatedly by at least five independent witnesses. "The figure was very tall, dressed in grey drapery. The drapery also partially enveloped the head, though allowing the features to be seen. The 'grey' was a light grey—perhaps such a colour as a white object would assume in partial darkness. The hands, it would seem, hung down and were clasped in front of the figure. The expression of the face was very calm and peaceful—a good face. . . . There was nothing indistinct about the outlines of the figure. The drapery was shapeless— that is, it had no definite shape, such as that of a dressing-gown or a monk's gown—but the lines of it were firm and clear. But the whole figure was shadowy and unsubstantial looking." There were sounds of footsteps, sighing, breathing, banging of doors (which were locked), draggings, etc., and a long account is given of the experiences of the various percipients.

After their seven years' tenancy was up, the family moved to another house in the neighbourhood. When they had been there about eighteen months, all the old noises started in the new house, increasing in intensity until they were as bad as ever. Then the same figure was seen. Here, then, is an example of a ghost which followed the family from one house to another.

The explanation which I suggest is that the ghost and the crisis-apparition are essentially the same type of phenomenon but sometimes the idea-pattern of the ghost inclines, in its content, towards that of the crisis-apparition.

## 6. THE POSSIBILITY OF COLLECTIVE "IDEA-PATTERNS"

It seems as if the more incoherent types of haunting were due to idea-patterns only very loosely connected, or perhaps not connected at all, with any idea in a conscious mind. One wonders whether such subconsciously initiated idea-patterns may in some cases be collective. If they were, they would throw light on many age-old traditions and legends. Popular tradition might supply material out of which such collective idea-patterns could be formed. Take, for example, the idea of the god Pan, half human and half goat-like, haunting certain places in the woods and uplands and playing his pipe. The widely spread idea that this happened might conceivably sink into the mid-levels of the personalities of a whole community, and there form a telepathic idea-pattern, having a multiple agency. Anyone (suitably sensitive) going to the places which, according to the idea-pattern, Pan was especially supposed to inhabit would then see and hear Pan with exactly the same reality that a person going into a haunted house sees and hears a ghost. And this would account for the firm belief in ancient times in the nature-gods; in Celtic and other countries in fairies, and so on. These people would believe in them because they really did see and hear them as one really does see and hear apparitions. There really would, on this view, be a reason for the universality, vitality, and permanence of these legends, which mere oral tradition scarcely seems enough to account for. This view is surely more convincing than the somewhat lame attempts of anthropologists to explain these things away. Collective and telepathically endowed idea-patterns would also explain epidemic appearances, for example, of the Virgin and the Saints in Catholic countries; the appearances of the Devil in the Middle Ages, and perhaps the sight of witches flying on broom-sticks and the metamorphosis of human beings into animals, etc. It may be that the Flying Dutchman has a similar explanation.

There seems, too, to be a possibility, even though a faint one, that the collective idea-pattern might bring some comfort to those who wish to escape from the necessity for attributing a survivalist agency to certain ghosts. Suppose that, during the life-time of a person whose ghost is seen to haunt the house after his death, a collective idea-pattern of him had been formed by the personalities of those who lived with him. This idea-pattern might have for its content the figure of the person moving about the house in his accustomed manner. After he died, therefore, these people might continue to see him; and strangers coming to the house would see him too, because of the telepathic character of the idea-pattern. The explanation seems to fail, however, in two ways. First, ghosts continue to haunt houses after the persons who lived with the prototype of the ghost have gone away or died. Secondly, there seems to be no reason why, if this explanation were true, the ghost should not haunt the house before the death of the person concerned as well as afterwards. The suggestion would, I think, only acquire plausibility in the case of some continuing and closed community, such as an abbey of monks, who might conceivably form such a collective idea-pattern with reference to a revered abbot. I have never heard of this kind of thing happening.

I have now done my best to consider what light the evidence for apparitions throws on their agency. The conclusion I reach is that if we consider all *recognized* apparitions, belonging to the four classes, as being the expressions of telepathic idea-patterns originating with the persons represented by the apparitions, we have the explanation which most naturally accords with the evidence, and which is also most economical of hypotheses. But it involves the admission that some ghosts and post-mortem cases, and probably some post-mortem crisis-cases, are due to surviving agents. If we reject survivalist agency on grounds independent of the evidence of psychical research, we must split our explanations up as follows. Classes (1) and (2), up to crises at the moment of death, would be explained as originated by living agents. Class (2) after death up to a period of 12 hours (which is quite an arbitrary period) as originated by living agents, but with telepathic deferment. Class (3) as due to subjective hallucination on the part of the percipient or percipients. Class (4) as due to some kind of physical traces left on the material of the haunted house; or to retrocognition; or to some kind of persistent image, etc. The chief objections to the latter method seem to be that: (*a*) it introduces a good deal of complication; (*b*) it introduces sharp divisions into the explanations where no sharp divisions appear in the evidence; (*c*) the evidence for telepathic deferment is by no means good; (*d*) some of the cases in Class (3) cannot be due to purely subjective hallucination because the apparition represents a recognized figure which was unknown to the percipient. Also, some of the cases are collective, and there is no independent evidence to show that subjective hallucinations are ever collective.

## 7. "OUT-OF-THE-BODY" EXPERIENCES

There is a small class of cases which, although they do not bear directly on the question of the agency of apparitions, are yet interesting and should be considered in connection with them. These are the cases in which persons who have nearly died have had experiences while in an apparently lifeless condition and have remembered them afterwards. Such experiences do not, of course, prove survival; but they are very surprising on an epiphenomenalist view of consciousness. CASE 57 Dr. Wiltse, of Skiddy, Kansas (the percipient in Case 9), lay ill with typhoid and subnormal temperature and pulse, felt himself to be dying, and said good-bye to his family and friends. He managed to straighten his legs and arrange his arms over his breast, and sank into utter unconsciousness. Dr. S. H. Raynes, the only physician present, said that he passed four hours without pulse or perceptible heart-beat. He was thought to be dead and the church bell was tolled. The doctor, however, thought he could perceive occasionally a very slight gasp; he thrust a needle into the flesh but got no response. The percipient, however, says that at last he again came into a state of conscious existence and found he was still in the body, "but the body and I no longer had any interests in common." He seemed to be getting out of his body, rocking to and fro and breaking connection with the body's tissues. He seemed to feel and hear the snapping of innumerable small cords and then, he says, "I began slowly to retreat from the feet, toward the head, as a rubber cord shortens." Presently he felt he was in the head and then emerging through the sutures of the skull. "I recollect distinctly," he continues, "how I appeared to myself something like a jellyfish as regards colour and form. As I emerged I saw two ladies sitting at my head. I measured the distances between the head of my cot and the knees of the lady opposite the head and concluded there was room for me to stand, but felt considerable embarrassment as I reflected that I was about to emerge naked before her. . . . As I emerged from the head I floated up and down and laterally like a soap-bubble attached to the bowl of a pipe until I at last broke loose from the body and fell lightly to the floor, where I slowly rose and expanded into the full stature of a man. I seemed to be translucent, of a bluish cast and perfectly naked." The percipient fled towards the door, but when he got there, found himself suddenly clothed, and his elbow came in contact with one of two men standing in the door-way (they were actually there) and to his surprise went through him without encountering any resistance. He tried to attract the attention of his friends but without success, so he walked out of the door and into the street. He says, "I never saw that street more distinctly than I saw it then. I took note of the redness of the soil and of the washes the rain had made." (There had been heavy rain and the roads were marked by rain-washes.) He then noticed that he was attached by means of a small cord, like a spider's web, to his body in the house, the cord coming from his shoulders. He then seemed to be propelled, as if by a pair of hands, and found himself on a roadway, while below him was a scene of mountain and forest which looked very like the local scenery. After various experiences he came to rocks blocking the road which he tried to climb round. But at that moment a black cloud descended on him; and he opened his eyes to find himself back in his sick-bed.

CASE 58 Another case, from Illinois, dates from the time of the American Civil War. The sergeant-major of a regiment of Volunteer Infantry was taken to hospital in a dying condition. "During all the afternoon," says the assistant surgeon, "he could only speak in whispers, and at 11 p.m. he to all appearance died. I was standing beside his father by the bed, and when we thought him dead the old man put forth his hand and closed the mouth of the corpse (?), and I, thinking he might faint in the keenness of his grief, said 'Don't do that! perhaps he will breathe again,' and immediately led him to a chair in the back part of the room, and returned, intending to bind up the fallen jaw and close the eyes myself. As I reached the bedside the supposed dead man looked suddenly up in my face and said, 'Doctor, what day of the month is it?' I told him the day of the month, and he answered, 'That is the day I died.' His father had sprung to the bedside, and turning his eyes on him, he said, 'Father, our boys have taken Fort Henry, and Charlie [his brother] isn't hurt. I've seen mother and the children, and they are well. He then gave quite comprehensive directions regarding his funeral. . . ." He again asked the date; said "That's the day I died," and instantly was dead.

The narrator adds that the fort was taken and the brother uninjured.

CASE 59 The next case is both uncorroborated and remote; but the narrator, the Rev. L. J. Bertrand, a Huguenot minister, gave his account verbally to Dr. Richard Hodgson and also sent a written account to Professor William James, from which the following is taken. The details may be inaccurate; but the main facts are likely to have been correctly remembered.

Mr. Bertrand had been accustomed for years to mountain climbing in the Alps and the Pyrenees. On this occasion he and his party decided, against the advice of the guides, to climb the Titlis on the difficult side from Engstlenalp, and when they reached the top of the steep and dangerous part they all felt surprised that they had not fallen, and Mr. Bertrand felt too tired to go on. He therefore decided to remain where he was and made the others promise to go up by the left and come down by the right. He continues, "I sat down, my legs hanging on a dangerous slope or precipice, my back leaning on a rock as big as an armchair. I chose that brink because there was no snow, and because I could face better the magnificent panorama of the Alpes Bernoises. I at once remembered that in my pocket were two cigars, and put one between my teeth, lighted a match, and considered myself as the happiest of men. Suddenly I felt as thunderstruck by apoplexy, and though the match burnt my fingers, I could not throw it down. My head was perfectly clear and healthy, but my body was as powerless and motionless as a rock. There was for me no hesitation. 'This,' I thought, *is the sleep of the snows!* If I move I shall roll down in the abyss; if I do not move I shall be a dead man in 25 or 30 minutes.' " He then describes how the cold of death crept upwards from his feet; how he felt an acute pain and seemed to die. Then he thought, "Well, at last I am what they call a dead man, and here I am, a ball of air in the air, a captive balloon still attached to earth by a kind of elastic string and going up and always up. [Compare Case 57, "I floated up and down and laterally like a soap-bubble."] How strange! I see better than ever, and I am dead—only a small space in the space without a body!" He then seemed to be able to follow the movements of the climbing party. He saw the guide going up by the right instead of by the left as he had promised; and he saw him lag behind and drink his bottle of Madeira and steal a leg of his chicken. When the party returned they managed to bring him back to life, and he charged the guide with these things, whereupon the man fled and spread the rumour that he was a devil and not a man!

CASE 60 The following case, which occurred during the 1914-18 War, was sent to Sir Oliver Lodge, and was copied by the narrator, Mr. Norman F. Ellison, from his War Diary. "We left Monchiet," he says, "in the early afternoon and after a gruelling march along a *pavé* road, slippery with mud and melted snow, reached Beaumetz at night. The briefest halt and then on to Wailly, immediately behind the line, some eight miles south of Arras. From there we waded through a winding communication trench a mile long but seemingly interminable. Liquid mud to the knees and a bitterly cold sleet benumbing us through. At last we reached the front line and took over from the French—a Territorial Reserve Battalion.

"The worst trenches we had ever been in. No repairs had been done to them for months and months. At worst, they had collapsed inwards and did not give head-shelter; at best they were a trough of liquid muck. H. and I in the same traverse and straight away on sentry duty. We were both too utterly fed up to even curse. Bodily exhausted, sodden and chilled to the bone with icy sleet, hungry and without rations or the means of lighting a fire to boil a dixey of water; not a dry square inch to sit upon, let alone a square foot of shelter beneath which to have the solace of a pipe, we agreed that this was the worst night of concentrated physical discomfort we had come across hitherto—and neither of us were strangers to discomfort.

"Several hours of this misery passed and then an amazing change came over me. I became conscious, acutely conscious, that I was outside myself; that the real 'me'—the Ego, spirit or what you like—was entirely separate and outside my fleshly body. I was looking, in a wholly detached and impersonal way, upon the discomforts of a khaki-clad body, which, whilst I realized that it was my own, might easily have belonged to somebody else for all the direct connection I seemed to have with it. I knew that my body must be feeling acutely cold and miserable, but I, my spirit part, felt nothing.

"At the time it seemed a very natural happening—as the impossibilities of a dream seem right and natural to the dreamer—and it was only afterwards that I came to the realization that I had been through one of the most wonderful experiences of my life.

"In the morning H. remarked to me upon my behaviour during the night. For a long time I had been grimly silent and then suddenly changed. My wit and humour under such trying circumstances, had amazed him. I had chatted away as unconcernedly as if we had been warm and comfortable before a roaring fire—'as if there was no war on' were his exact words, I remember.

"I never mentioned a word to H. or to anybody else about

my spiritual adventure that night. He would not have understood and would have laughed at it all, but nothing will shake
my inward belief and knowledge that on this particular night
my soul and body were entirely separated from each other."

CASE 61  The last instance of these experiences is not one
of the S.P.R.'s cases, but seems nevertheless to be well worth
quoting. Sir Alexander Ogston, K.C.V.O., records that he had,
at the time of the South African War, been admitted to
Bloemfontein Hospital suffering from typhoid fever. "In my
delirium," he says, "night and day made little difference to
me. In the four-bedded ward where they first placed me, I
lay, as it seemed, in a constant stupor which excluded the
existence of any hopes or fears. Mind and body seemed
to be dual, and to some extent separate. I was conscious of
the body as an inert, tumbled mass near a door; it belonged
to me, but it was not *I*. I was conscious that my mental self
used regularly to leave the body, always carrying something
soft and black, I did not know what, in my left hand—that
was invariable—and wander away from it under grey, sun-
less, moonless, starless skies, ever onwards to a distant gleam
on the horizon, solitary but not unhappy, and seeing other
dark shades gliding silently by until something produced a
consciousness that the chilly mass, which I then recalled was
my body, was being stirred as it lay by the door. I was then
drawn rapidly back to it, joined it with disgust, and it became
*I* and was fed, spoken to and cared for. When it was again
left I seemed to wander off as before by the side of a dark,
slowly flowing, great flood through silent fields of asphodel,
knowing neither light nor darkness, and though I knew that
death was hovering about, having no thought of religion nor
dread of the end, and roamed on beneath the murky skies
apathetic and contented, until something again disturbed the
body where it lay, when I was drawn back to it afresh and
entered it with ever-growing repulsion. As the days went
on, or rather, I should say, as time passed, all I knew of my
sickness was that the wanderings through the dim asphodel
fields became more continual and more distinct, until about
the end of the term of high fever I was summoned back to
the huddled mass with intense loathing, and as I drew near
and heard some one say, 'He will live,' I remembered finding

the mass less cold and clammy, and ever after that the wanderings appeared to be fewer and shorter, the thing lying at the door and I grew more together, and ceased to be separated into two entities.

"In my wanderings there was a strange consciousness that I could see through the walls of the building, though I was aware that they were there and that everything was transparent to my senses. I saw plainly, for instance, a poor R.A.M.C. surgeon, of whose existence I had not known, and who was in quite another part of the hospital, grow very ill and scream and die; I saw them cover his corpse and carry him softly out on shoeless feet, quietly and surreptitiously, lest we should know that he had died, and the next night I thought take him away to the cemetery. Afterwards when I told these happenings to the sisters, they informed me that all this had happened just as I had fancied. . . .

"Towards the middle of June, or possibly somewhat earlier, before I was well conscious, there was a consultation, and one elderly doctor shook his head and said so that I could hear it, 'He is nearly sixty, he won't recover.' Another said, 'He'll get better,' and it confusedly amazed me, for I knew perfectly that I should get well. . . ."

## Chapter VI

## Speculation and Reflection

THE STUDY OF APPARITIONS is now seen to throw light in two directions into the recesses of human personality. (1) It throws light on the *modus operandi* of hallucinations, and (2) it throws light on the structure of personality by revealing that apparitions are the sensory expression of dramatic constructs, created in regions of the personality outside the field of normal consciousness.

### 1. HOW FAR CAN SENSORY HALLUCINATIONS GO?

First, with regard to telepathic hallucinations, in his Presidential Address to the Society for Psychical Research Professor Price encouraged us to be bold in speculation though careful in collecting facts. I am going to follow the first item of his advice and speculate boldly—some may say wildly—about apparitions. In the first place I would draw attention to the extremely unpromising conditions under which apparitions occur. An ordinary human being passes through a brief period of crisis and another ordinary human being simultaneously undergoes an experience of pseudo-perception. No particularly sensitive persons are involved; no specially helpful conditions are provided; yet the pseudo-perception or hallucination is often so good an imitation of a material figure as to be at first mistaken for it; and sometimes the unusual clarity of the figure is remarked upon. It is difficult to refrain from asking what sort of hallucinations would take place if the conditions were more favourable. Even as it is, the three senses of sight, touch, and hearing are all hallucinated, and there is some evidence that the senses of taste and smell can be hallucinated also. In principle, therefore, telepathic hallucinations are remarkably complete, though on actual occasions they are somewhat scrappy and fleeting. What would happen if the conditions were much better and remained relatively permanent?

I have supposed that apparitions are caused by the existence of "idea-patterns" constructed jointly by mid-level constituents of the personality, which are concerned in the theme or pattern, and expressed by other mid-level constituents, which are able to generate the necessary sense-imagery. Let us suppose that such an idea-pattern, instead of arising from momentary activity on the part of two or three individuals, were impressed on a large group of individuals by some mind or personality of a very powerful kind, acting on them all. One might suppose it to be by some demiurge. Each member of the group would play his part in the theme of the idea-pattern, so that the net result would be that the whole group of persons would appear to themselves to be living in whatever environment the idea-pattern impressed on them. They would be in a complete though hallucinatory world. It is true that as long as these persons possessed material bodies, the hallucination would not be quite complete. It would have to compete with the physical world revealed to them by their physical senses, rather as Mr. A.'s hallucinatory world did in Case 35. In particular, they would be able to prove the hallucinatory or non-physical character of this impressed world by passing through its visual solids. But if we take a further step and suppose these persons to have shed their physical bodies, without having otherwise changed their personalities, then this impressed, hallucinatory world would have no competitor. Everything in it would behave *as if* all were physically occupied. The group of persons would, in fact, appear to themselves to be living in a physical world; and there would seem to be no test by which they could tell whether their world were physical or hallucinatory. A point to be noticed about such a world is that it would not be purely subjective: it would be based upon something existing independently of the percipients, but that something would not be physical substance: it would be an all-pervasive idea-pattern. Whether such a world should be called hallucinatory or not is merely a matter of terminology. The world experienced by this supposed group of percipients would be extraordinarily near to a Berkeleian world, the independent factor in it being something which might, in picturesque metaphor, be called "thoughts in the mind of God." It may be said that it is utterly fantastic to suggest that hallucinations could ever become so comprehensive or so complete; or that they could ever provide a sensory world replete in every detail and perfect in every action. That may or may not be the case; but the most extraordinary thing about sensory hallucinations is the perfect correlation of detail which they show and their almost uncanny imitation of physical objects. Where, exactly, does this semi-miraculous power of imitation stop? Moreover, the correlation can be carried out collectively. How do we know that there is an upper limit to the number of persons who can be collectively hallucinated?

There is another feature of great interest about such a

supposed hallucinatory world. It was pointed out in connection with Case 12 that it is possible for a percipient to be perceptually aware of *two* three-dimensional spaces at once, *which have no spatial relation to one another*. The group of persons I have supposed to be under the influence of this general idea-pattern would be perceptually aware of a space (which they, no doubt, would call "physical space"); and this would be spatially unrelated to what *we* call "physical space." And for every such comprehensive idea-pattern there could be a separate sensible space; in fact there could be any number of three-dimensional spaces co-existing without having anything, spatially, to do with one another. We catch a glimpse here of the far-reaching principle that a "perceived" space might be indistinguishable from physical space so far as the hypothetical observer of such a space is concerned. And any world existing in such a "perceived" space might seem as real to an observer of it as our own physical world is to ourselves. Yet neither such a "perceived" space nor such a "perceived" world, although both would be dependent in part on the observer, would be purely subjective. Both would contain an element independent of the observer and would possess as much objectivity as our own physical world possesses, so far as any dweller in such a world could discover. The question of "where" another three-dimensional space could be simply disappears and becomes meaningless. This forms an example of a principle revealed by psychical research, about which more will be said presently, namely that an inquiry into human personality is likely to shed light on a good many problems besides the nature of personality itself. If problems about space are mooted, people turn at once to geometry. It seems that it may be more enlightening to turn to the observer. These suppositional spaces provide a universe with plenty of room in it. And there would seem to be no reason why a comprehensive idea-pattern should copy the theme of the physical world. There is room for any amount of variation.

Whether anything analogous could happen in the case of time I do not know. Time does not enter into the subject-matter of the present survey.

## 2. THE CLASH BETWEEN "MID-LEVEL" PROCESSES AND COMMON-SENSE REALISM

With regard to the light thrown by apparitions on the structure of personality, the apparitional constructs have been called "idea-patterns"; and since the idea-pattern must be constructed by someone or something, and since also it is clearly expressed by someone or something, I have postulated certain levels within the personality supposed to be responsible for performing these functions, and have called them, metaphorically, the "producer" of the drama and the "executor" or "stage-carpenter" respectively. Of course, this metaphor is not to be taken literally. The producer and stage-carpenter are not persons: they are psychological or quasi-psychological constituents of the personality—factors in a complex organization such as the human personality evidently is; and they must possess characteristics very unlike those of anything we meet with in the sensible world—characteristics which lie intermediately between those of body and those of self. In fact, body and self would appear to be the lower and upper limits of a personality in which the producer and the stage-carpenter are only two out of, probably, a host of elements.

It is difficult to picture the characteristics of such intermediate factors of the personality because the mind is adapted to think in terms of the material environment or concepts largely based upon it. We tend to think that every new thing we come across must necessarily be derived from matter, and find it hard to imagine that it may possess non-matter-like qualities intrinsically and in its own right. This habitual view makes consciousness or pure Self an anomaly which has to be explained away as far as possible or ignored, as it is in Behaviourist psychology, or belittled in one way or another. Thus Whitehead says somewhere, "Consciousness seems to count for very little"; Alexander says, "Consciousness or . . . 'mentality' is a quality of a neural process"; and Santayana says that consciousness "is a mere play on the surface of things." This outlook, which is embarrassed by the fact of consciousness, must, I think, be based on a naïve acceptance of the world as presented by sense-perception; although the acceptance is not so much conscious and intellectual as subconscious and psychological. This is why philosophers and ordinary men are equally prone to it. And, of course, where there is no room for consciousness, there is none either for such psychological factors of personality as we are postulating.

The view of personality to which our researches point is more nearly like that which Professor William McDougall outlined in his Presidential Address to the Society for Psychical Research, delivered in 1920—the view that personality is a graded hierarchy. If anything like this view be true, we are missing our opportunities by looking *through* our personalities into the external world for enlightenment instead of looking *at* them; and then framing theories about personality based on what we see when we look *through* it. As has been said, we are in a position of a person looking through a pair of field-glasses, who may go on looking day after day without even getting an inkling of how the optical magnification he uses is achieved. For that he must take them to pieces and look *at* them.

The Society has now made careful observations and experiments on various manifestations of the human personality extending over a period of sixty years; but the intellectual world is not impressed. There is, I think, a suspicion beginning to dawn on the scientific mind, as a result of long hammering, that there may be a new and strange faculty of human perception called "telepathy"; but the idea that, through the study of human personality, our whole conception of the nature of things may undergo a radical change is as far as ever from making its appearance in the philosophical and scientific worlds. But the attitude of the world, though disappointing, is nevertheless instructive. I am not going to upbraid our critics for their indifference; but it may be opportune to glance for a moment at their attitude in order to consider whether it should influence our future policy.

On the whole, as I have said, our work appears to have evoked a reaction of indifference tinged with contempt. In no quarter has the keen, exploring spirit been shown—the spirit anxious to learn all the subject has to reveal. Our work has been almost studiously ignored, such criticism as has been meted out having taken the form of *escapist* tactics. And this, it seems to me, should teach us a good deal; for the reason alleged, namely that our evidence is too poor and meagre to merit attention, is not, I believe, the true one. The true reason is that all the facts we have brought to light clash violently with a widely accepted view about the nature of things. You cannot take facts like telepathy or precognition and simply tack them on to this accepted outlook. Telepathy demands a revolution in current ideas about human personality; and precognition demands a revolution in current ideas about time. In general, the entire outlook necessitated by the findings of psychical research breaks up the naïve realism in which the human mind is steeped and shows it to be largely illusory; and I suggest that the distaste for psychical phenomena is mainly due to a half-unconscious instinct which prompts people to rally in defence of common-sense realism. It is, in a sense, a reaction to defend a *creed*. We most of us feel in our bones that whatever castles the intellect may build in moments of abstraction or whatever direction theory may take a part from the activities of daily life—whatever queer facts, even, may occasionally come to light—common sense still remains the final guide to truth. That is why people "recover" so quickly from cogent psychical evidence and even, sometimes, from psychical experiences of their own; and why they "recover" from the arguments of philosophy and religion as soon as they get back into the everyday world. People are not nearly so fastidious about logical standards of proof in other matters as they pretend to be in psychical matters; but their attitude does not really arise from any extreme respect for logic, but from a fear that psychical evidence will lead them, to use a colloquialism, "up the garden path." They think that if they once admit this evidence it will plunge them headlong back into superstition and wreck the structure of law on which science has been built. They think, as one psychologist put it, that it is a case of psychical research alive and science dead, or *vice versa*.

The situation is not altogether easy to describe, but it

appears to be more or less as follows. The world in which we live and act is revealed to us by our physical sense-organs, and we are *adapted* to this world mentally, psychologically, and physically, so that the literal and unquestioning belief we have in it is not so much an intellectual opinion as an organic conviction which nature has instilled into us with all the force of an inculcated *suggestion*. We are impregnated with it down to the core of our being. It is in the blood rather than in the mind. Yet when we bring reason to bear on this conviction we are forced to admit that it is largely an illusion. (The whole philosophy of F. H. Bradley illustrates the point.) It is only necessary to ask enough questions about almost anything that appears "obvious" to common sense for that "obviousness" to fade away. We have already had to ask whether, when we meet a person in the flesh, his conscious self is present in space where his body is. To common sense it "obviously" is; but we found that the proposition had no clear meaning when looked into. Or one may question the "obvious" view of time. The world has ceased to exist in the past and does not yet exist in the future. "Obviously" it only exists at the present moment. But the present moment is a dimensionless instant with no room in it for anything to happen; so that what is "obviously" true is also nonsense. We have already seen what a perplexing puzzle the "simple and obvious" world of the senses becomes directly we begin to analyse it. The fact is that common sense only works for the practical purposes of daily life, for which it is intended; and a struggle arises between one view of things which is *psychologically* ingrained into us and quite a different view which is the result of reflective *reason*.

Psychical research provides evidence for facts which are completely unassimilable by the psychologically ingrained view (which is much the most powerful with every human being, be he philosopher or dustman), and that is why people try to reject them. Before we can realize that psychical facts fit naturally in the complete scheme of things we must realize also that this psychologically ingrained view does not tell us the ultimate truth about the world, but is a peculiar system of appearances got up to serve a practical end.

### 3. A QUESTION OF POLICY

The question which arises, therefore, is whether it is any use continuing to amass evidence only, and whether we must not at the same time show people that there is a rational way of accepting it. It is of course a large order to educate our critics as well as supplying them with evidence! But I think we might make a useful beginning by educating ourselves in a certain sense, that is to say, by building up a theory at the same time that we collect our facts. We need to try to *explain* our facts as best we can as we go along. My suggestion is that *our first and most vital step should be to form new qualitative ideas about the elements and processes of personality by an intensive study of our evidence.* Once some idea has been gained about what is going on in the personality, a good deal of light may be expected to shine on collateral problems as well, such as the nature of space and time, and perhaps of the material world as a whole. Having studied the existing evidence, we should go further and plan experiment with the primary aim of obtaining still more light on the workings of personality. The most important field to study would seem to be that of trance, hypnotic, hypnoidal, and automatic states; our aim should be, by selecting the right subjects and forming the right investigating groups, to raise automatic and trance material to the highest possible pitch of quality and coherence and then to subject the material to rigorous psychological analysis. If, as seems likely, such trance and automatic material should be found to consist of psychological constructs or idea-patterns attaining their final expression in verbal form, each such construct should be treated as an item of raw material to be examined for the internal evidence it contains, not only of agency, but also of construction and mode of expression. This was to a considerable extent the work aimed at by the "Cross-correspondences," and in particular by the automatic script of Mrs. Willett, which seemed in itself to be trying to assist the investigator to obtain this kind of information. Again, Mr. Kenneth Richmond gave an excellent example of how to deal with trance-productions of the more ordinary kind from this point of view in his psychological examination of the Leonard material.[1]

On the more directly experimental side the same principle suggests that we should direct our main effort towards a thorough exploration of hypnotic and similar states, testing the scope of hypnotic sensory hallucinations and trying, under hypnosis, or some allied state, to produce extra-sensory perception. Hypnosis has been approached by psychologists mainly from the therapeutic standpoint and seems never to have been explored from the point of view of psychical research. With the example before us of the type of sensitives described in Chapter IV, we should surely try to combine hypnosis with the selection of suitable subjects. Work on extra-sensory perception under such conditions should provide far better material than can be obtained by tapping average samples of the public, and would dispense with the need for a laborious and cumbersome statistical technique.

The quantitative methods of research on which we are now concentrating, although useful and perhaps indispensable for the solution of certain problems, are in many ways very unsuitable for psychical research, the main features of which are *qualitative* and slip through the quantitative net. It is often said it is a great advantage to be able to quote a figure with reference to chance-coincidence instead of merely saying, "It is extremely improbable." But there are two remarks to be made about this. One is that the advantage of being able to quote a figure disappears if it is obvious to common sense that the figure would be nowhere near the point of significance (and it is only near it if one is dealing with poor material). The other is that the very precision of a numerical result introduces a danger because, although the result of the experiment, expressed in figures, is always perfectly definite, it does not follow that the meaning of the result need be equally definite. In a mathematical method the meaning of the result depends entirely on the assumptions which have been made before the mathematics were applied. Unless these are crystal clear, the definiteness of the numerical result may be a delusion and a snare. There is, for example, the danger of dealing with false classes, which was pointed out in Chapter

[1] *Proc.* xliv. 19-52.

III. If two classes of phenomena, which may have a superficial resemblance, but which have also essential differences, are grouped together as one class for the purposes of a statistical calculation, the result of the calculation will show a perfectly definite figure; but it is almost certain that this figure will be assumed to mean what it does not. The danger of making cloudy assumptions is, I think, considerably greater in psychical research than in biology, sociology, and physics —the sciences in which statistical methods have been conspicuously useful and successful. For psychical phenomena are eminently lacking in uniformity and are rich in qualitative differences. It seems to me, therefore, that the quantitative method should be regarded as a useful auxiliary, but that our main effort should be concentrated on qualitative research.

It is often said that the great desideratum for psychical research is to bring its phenomena under experimental control, and the employment of quantitative methods is sometimes supposed to be the best way of doing this. There is, no doubt, much truth in the demand for experimental control; but I think also a certain amount of misapprehension. For those who say this have their eye on the cut-and-dried experimental methods of the physical sciences. But psychical research is in a very different position from physics and is a very different type of inquiry. It is unexplored, virgin territory in a sense in which the physical sciences are not. We are eminently pioneers. These people want to build a railway, whereas our first duty is to make a rough map of the terrain. We have, I feel sure, to begin by forming *new ideas* about it. These ideas will be qualitative and very new, and probably very upsetting to common sense and logic. Without them we shall make no progress but shall only go on reshuffling old material endlessly.

The repeatability of an experiment is often spoken of nowadays as if it were bound up with statistical methods. Strictly speaking, most of the past work, apart from the spontaneous cases, is repeatable—experiments in automatic writing, booktests, newspaper tests, sittings with mediums, and so on. One outstandingly important experiment in telepathy—the experimental production of apparitions, which has already been successfully done sixteen times—is definitely repeatable; yet for some reason nobody ever repeats it, although this experiment might be expected to throw light both on telepathy and on the nature of apparitions. The word "repeatable" (besides, perhaps, meaning *easily* repeatable) seems to be used to mean, simultaneously, two things: (1) an experiment which can be relied upon to give the same result every time it is tried, and (2) an experiment of the same type as those familiar in physical science. The first seems to be very desirable, provided it is compatible with the pioneering technique needed for exploration. And it is a desideratum to have an experiment of this kind up one's sleeve, so to speak, for demonstration purposes. But I do not think it is the kind of experiment to which we should tie ourselves down. The second point, in my view, has no justification.

### 4. BEARING OF THE EVIDENCE ON SURVIVAL

The question of the agency of apparitions has been considered above, but there is an important general principle which should be borne in mind in relation to the question of whether psychical evidence can prove survival: and, indeed, this principle is involved in most of the questions raised by psychical research. The principle has already been touched on in Chapter III. It is this: The possibility of getting an answer to a question depends on the background of thought which is assumed when the question is asked. The questioner always has in mind a particular background of thought in terms of which he expects the answer to his question to be given; and it may be that as long as he holds this background of thought, no answer is possible. It is because of the lack of adequate background that religious and mystical experiences, however great their importance, have to remain, for the most part, the incommunicable possessions of individuals. The main thing to bear in mind is that the background *conditions* the possible answers to questions. There is, for example, the perennial problem of whether the hen or the egg came first. There is an assumed background to this question without which it would not be a sensible question at all. The background is the assumption that either the hen or the egg must have appeared on the scene suddenly. Seen against the background of evolution, which is of course the true one, we find that the hen and the egg were both developed gradually from ancestors, which become more and more unlike them the further we go back. There was never a moment when there was a first hen's egg or a first hen; and against this background the question loses its point.

In the case of most great questions it is the background which counts. It may be worth while to illustrate this in the case of the dispute about survival by quoting some of the commonest *a priori* objections to it. When these objections are raised, the questioner almost invariably has in mind a background of thought, which it will be convenient to call the "common-sense outlook." The slight glimpse we have so far achieved shows that personality possesses mid-level elements which cannot be grasped by common-sense ideas, and which therefore lie outside this common-sense outlook. At the start, therefore, the way lies open to misunderstanding: for it can scarcely be denied that the question of survival and the nature of personality are intimately connected. These mid-levels, as soon as we catch sight of them, present the most baffling problems to common sense. They differ from one another in function and character without showing any clear numerical separation. They sweep away the idea of a clear-cut Self (one kind of thing) inhabiting a clear-cut Body (another kind of thing). Instead, they invite us to contemplate a personality *informed* by Selfhood, but informed by it, in respect of its "levels," in varying degrees. This is a baffling conception. The personality is in some sense hierarchical, and the higher we go in the hierarchy, the more self-like the levels of the hierarchy become and at the same time the more impossible for our minds to grasp. The lower we go in the hierarchy, the less self-like the levels become and the nearer to numerically separate units. The mid-levels, therefore, can be regarded as an *internal environment* to pure Self from one point of view and as *being* that Self from another. The idea of selfhood *in degree* is very strange to common habits of thought. Yet it seems to hold down to the lowest level of the personality, the Body. This has already been pointed out in Chapter III.

When considering the pros and cons of survival, it makes all the difference what view of personality is assumed as the background of the questions. I do not mean to say that the bare question, Do we or do we not survive death? has no meaning if asked against the common-sense background. Clearly it has, for the negative answer at least is definite (although I do not think it is quite so definite or clear if subjected to a close analysis as it appears to be on the surface). But a positive answer almost certainly introduces at once false or misleading ideas. The only kind of survival we can envisage clearly in common-sense terms is a perpetuation of the life we now enjoy, or endure; and it is possible that this does not help us very much. The common-sense view of time must be utterly inadequate: the evidence for precognition warns us of that: and the nature of time is relevant in any view of an extra-terrestrial existence. Thus, it is quite on the cards that when discussing survival we may involve ourselves in questions as unanswerable as that of the hen and the egg.

Professor E. R. Dodds, in an interesting paper entitled "Why I do not believe in Survival," dealt with certain *a priori* objections to it.[2] I will summarize the most important of them very briefly, omitting those connected with ethics and religion.

In the first place, Professor Dodds pointed out that the theory of survival appears to involve that of pre-existence; and pre-existence raises at least three unsolved difficulties. (1) Besides the factors of heredity and environment, there must, in the human being, be a third factor, namely the pre-existent self, of which psychologists have found no trace. (2) On the theory of pre-existence, the newborn infant must be a mature mind, whereas it appears to be simply an infant mind in an infant body. (3) There must be some mechanism of incarnation which lacks even the remotest biological analogue. Now, most of the apparent cogency of these objections arises from the assumption, quite natural to common sense, that all that a human being is must appear on the surface—the assumption, in fact, that a human being is simply a conscious mind tacked on to a material body. But if the human being is the vastly complex structure that psychical

[2] *Proc.* xlii. pp. 147-72.

research is beginning to reveal (and not merely complex, but, as regards its higher phases, impenetrable to thought and of unknown profundity), there may surely be a great deal of it which does not show. In fact, it may well be only a specialized part of it that does show. Seen against this background, the three objections to pre-existence raise, to say the least of it, a good deal less difficulty than they do when seen against the background of common sense. There may well be a third factor, a pre-existing self; in fact, there may well be many factors in the subtly woven personal complex, of whose independent existence we can see no trace from without.

Another objection mentioned by Professor Dodds changes its complexion when we begin to grasp the nature of the idea-pattern. Communications ostensibly proceeding from the dead, he says, have never been convincing. They have communicated nothing of value, and have been susceptible of different explanations at different times—as originated by gods or demons in Graeco-Roman times; by the Devil in medieval times; and by departed human beings in modern times. Their validity is therefore seriously impugned. Again, the point of the objection lies in the assumption of the common-sense background that these are straightforward communications from one being to another, in the mode of human intercourse. If, however, these are not communications but idea-patterns, jointly constructed by the personalities of the living persons concerned, it is scarcely surprising that they should be coloured by the prevailing ideas of the age. On this view they are local *vehicles* only, and the question of whether or not a discarnate agency is inspiring them is still an open one.

A final question asked by Professor Dodds is how, if the mind decays with the body in old age, it can be expected to survive it. This question is, of course, bound up with the general question of psycho-physical interdependence; but the same principle is involved. The cogency of the question depends, as before, on the assumption having been made that a human being is merely a psycho-physical compound—as if it consisted solely of a conscious mind controlling a material body. In the light of the view of personality now unfolding, the point of the argument becomes less obvious, and the argument itself needs to be much more carefully stated; for it is not clear that the pure self, as distinct from certain psychological elements of the personality, decays.

These questions may perhaps serve to illustrate my point, which is that as long as we ask questions in terms of an inadequate background of thought we shall continue to receive misleading answers. If we insist on asking these questions (and people do insist), we must first devote our energies to the attainment of an adequate background. The way to attain such a background is quite obviously to study human personality.

Whether psychical research has given reasonable ground for either a positive or negative conclusion regarding survival must, of course, be a matter for individual judgement. It has often been questioned whether positive proof is possible. If I may speak personally, I would say that it seems to me that the crude question has been rubbed off the slate (for the very reason of inadequate background), and instead of a direct answer we have had revealed to us something of the general perspective in which the question ought to be asked. We have been shown, in fact, that new conceptions must be grasped before the question can be intelligibly answered. But I think we can say that if the reply had been a simple negative, the vistas of personality now gradually unfolding before us would not have been found to exist. Psychical research has certainly not drawn a blank. It has, on the contrary, discovered something so big that people sheer away from it in a reaction of fear. They feel that they cannot cope with it, and are unwilling to make the drastic overhaul of their cherished convictions which the subject demands.

Psychical research, conducted by a mere handful of explorers working under difficulties, has not been able, up to the present, to influence the scientific and educated world to see the importance of the subject or to see it in its true light. The cult of popular Spiritualism, which is our worst enemy, unfortunately serves to increase this misunderstanding and mistrust. But in spite of our difficulties, we have gone far enough to feel sure that we have embarked on a rich field of discovery. If a weighty body of people now existed, sufficiently detached from worldly interests and sufficiently enthusiastic to make a great effort to obtain light on the Human

Situation—on the questions of What we are, Why we are, and Where we are—it is probable that psychical research could do more permanent good for mankind, struggling in its present quagmire, than all the schemes of social reconstruction, necessary as these are. For the world seems to have reached a stage in which belief in the value of the individual can no longer be sustained by the forces of religion and morality alone, but needs the backing of an intellectual conviction based on direct exploration of the human being.

# Appendix

## List of Principal Cases, with Sources

### EXAMPLES OF ABBREVIATIONS

*Proc.* viii. 311 = *Proceedings* of the Society for Psychical Research, Volume viii, page 311.

*J.* vi. 230 = *Journal* of the Society for Psychical Research, Volume vi, page 230.

*P.L.* (34) = *Phantasms of the Living*, by E. Gurney, F. W. H. Myers, and F. Podmore, Case 34.

*H.P.* (714) = *Human Personality and its Survival of Bodily Death*, by F. W. H. Myers, Case 714.

Page references are to the original editions of these works.

*Expectancy* (p. 28)
  Case 1.  *P.L.* I. p. 270
  Case 2.  *P.L.* (127)
*Experimental Case* (pp. 36-7-8)
  Case 3.  *P.L.* (15)
*Crisis Case* (p. 39)
  Case 4.  *Proc.* xxxiii. 170
*Post-mortem Case* (pp. 39-40)
  Case 5.  *Proc.* vi. 26
*Ghost* (pp. 41-2)
  Case 6.  *Proc.* iii. 102
*Spatial Presentation* (pp. 53-8)
  Case 7.  *P.L.* (220)
  Case 8.  *P.L.* (223)
  Case 9.  *Proc.* xi. 573
  Case 10.  *Proc.* x. 371
  Case 11.  *P.L.* (331)
  Case 12.  *Proc.* vii. 32
  Case 13.  *P.L.* (65)
  Case 14.  *Proc.* viii. 218
*Non-physical Character* (pp. 58-65)

Case 15.  *P.L.* (34)
Case 16.  *Proc.* viii. 311
Case 18.  *P.L.* (682)
Case 19.  *P.L.* I. p. 517 n.
Case 20.  *J.* vi. 135
*Imitation of Normal Perception* (pp. 65-72)
Case 21.  *P.L.* (254)
Case 22.  *J.* xx. 78
Case 23.  *J.* v. 10
Case 24.  *P.L.* (210)
Case 25.  *Proc.* v. 437
Case 26.  *J.* v. 224
Case 27.  *J.* vi. 145
Case 28.  *Proc.* xi. 445
Case 29.  *J.* vii. 26
*Additional Features* (pp. 72-6)
Case 30.  *P.L.* (264)
Case 31.  Sir Ernest Bennett, *Apparitions and Haunted Houses*, Case 102
Case 32.  *J.* vi. 129
Case 33.  *P.L.* (665)

189

# Index